Is The ELCA *Lutheran?*

What do you think
they'll replace it with?

Is The ELCA *Lutheran?*

Christine Larsen Goble

Elderberry Press, LLC
OAKLAND

Elderberry Press, LLC
1393 Old Homestead Drive, Second floor
Oakland, Oregon 97462—9506.
E-MAIL: editor@elderberrypress.com
TEL/FAX: 541.459.6043
www.elderberrypress.com

All Elderberry books are available from your favorite bookstore, amazon.com, or from our 24 hour order line: 1.800.431.1579

Library of Congress Control Number: 2004115944
Publisher's Catalog—in—Publication Data
Is The ELCA Lutheran? /Christine Larsen Goble
ISBN 1932762272
1. Lutheran.
2. Christianity.
3. Church.
4. Religion.
5. Martin Luther.
I. Title.

This book was written, printed and bound in the United States of America.

The author is grateful to Dr. Miles Olson for reading, editing and commenting extensively and helpfully on the draft, to Dr. Meg Madson who did the best she could to clean up the theology, and to Pastors Luther Bergeland and Bruce Bergquist for reading and providing helpful suggestions, and for their encouragement. Most of all I thank George who listened critically to every word, more than once. Thank you all. The content, now that it is done, is my own fault.

Table of Contents

Foreword....9
What's Going On in My Church?....11
Can We Talk?....19
Why Do They Want It?....25
The House with the Orange Door....27
We'll See—A Commentary on ELCA Top-Down Management....35
The CCM: Not Your Ordinary Ecumenical Agreement....39
The Good, the Bad and the Ugly: Sex and the Church....49
Especially about the Future....75
Diversity: the Goal that Morphs....89
Where Did All the Daddies Go?....99
Hymns in Our Hearts....103
As Others See Us....107
What Do Lutherans Believe?....113
I Want to Do It Myself!....133
Rules and Regs....137
My Word!....139
A World Full of Feelings....143
Good Work(s)....147
What If?....151
Is the ELCA Lutheran?....155
Up Close and Personal....161
Resources for Further Study....167
Appendix A....179
Resolutions Currently Circulating....179
Marriage and Family Resolution....185
Appendix B....189
The Church I Grew Up In....189

Foreword

I am writing this book to make the case that the Lutheran faith is a treasure worth saving, and that there is a real danger that in its largest organization in the U. S., the Evangelical Lutheran Church in America (ELCA), it is abandoning its central mission. I hope its readers will become part of a great groundswell of Lutheran conviction and determination to reclaim the Lutheran faith in an institution faithful to scripture and Lutheran theology, and thus faithful to those of us who are a part of the Lutheran church.

As you will see, the book is a collection of essays, short and long. In content and purpose they vary a great deal, but the intent behind them is to present, in this varied way, serious food for thought about our church.

When I initiated a discussion at my church on the issues of the CCM (Call to Common Mission) and later on the ELCA's activities related to the homosexuality and marriage controversies, I was met with open-mouthed amazement. Many thought such problems are Episcopal or Roman Catholic problems—not Lutheran problems. Fellow members told me that their cousins, children and hometown friends around the country were equally uninformed. Of those who were aware, some were uncomfortable, some downright angry that the issues were being raised, publicly, congregation-wide.

It appears to me that the ELCA is quietly accomplishing a mini-revolution in Lutheran practice. They are counting on the general reluctance of the clergy to address any potentially divisive issue with their members, and the sleepy confidence of members that everything is going to be all right in the end. One day we'll wake up and it will be a done deal. Yet there is enough coverage of the issues in *The Lutheran* magazine and other media that the ELCA cannot be accused of maintaining a blackout. Our congregation has not subscribed to *The Lutheran* for a long time. It caused too many telephone calls to the church office every time an issue hit the mailboxes, which tells you something.

Never discount the power of our natural reluctance to engage in controversy, especially about topics that are potentially embarrassing. We don't want to hurt anyone's feelings or jeopardize our relationships by disagreements. Cultural relativism and political correctness have dampened everyone's enthusiasm for a good bull session. It is a timid time inside the church. Yet we are not all quiet and wobbly. The Lutheran church historically has pointed to Jesus Christ very effectively and powerfully. We are heirs of a cohesive body of belief and a rich tradition of teaching scripture and the basic tenets of our faith. Some of us are blessed not only with a powerful faith, but with courage as well. We're going to need it.

Christine Larsen Goble, September 2004

What's Going On in My Church?

Some years ago I read the Cadfael mysteries by Ellis Peters—all twenty of them, one after another. It was like eating fresh plums, and then the bowl was empty and I wished there were just one more. The Cadfael mysteries are set in Shropshire, England, in the west, near the Welsh border. The time is the Twelfth Century. That was the time of the wars between Stephen and his cousin Matilda for the throne of England, a bloody, unsettled time of intrigue and betrayal in high places. As always, it was also a time of striving and labor, living and dying, marrying and giving birth, seedtime and harvest and picking up the pieces by the ordinary folk. It was a time when it was both necessary and dangerous to take sides.

Brother Cadfael, the holy sleuth of the tales, had a simple and profound Christian faith in a culture and at a time when Christianity permeated every closet and workshop of life. That is what struck me most forcefully about the books—that, and the fact that wherever Cadfael was, somebody was sure to be snuffed out before the third chapter. The twelfth century was hardly a provincially narrow or idyllic time. Cadfael himself had gone all the way to Jerusalem with the Crusades. Monasteries were busy inns for travelers, hospitals for the sick and hiding places for misfits. Barons were jockeying for power in the new government, whatever that should turn out to be, and clergy were doing the same. Christianity was the norm and the rule, through it all.

To say that the culture was Christian, bone and marrow, is not to say that everyone in it was a believer. Nor was it true then, if ever, that every Christian went about his business the very picture of Christian charity, piety and good will. Four hundred years later, Martin Luther would say that we who are saved are all saints, all sinners at the same time. It is a truth so obvious to introspection, so easy to forget.

A part of me longs for the security and assurance that such a culture provides. It was a civilization more certain of its moorings than ours. There was a prevailing faith, a common standard of right and wrong and a common view of responsibility and judgment. One could speak God's name confidently, without defending the right to do so. Loving and serving Christ, while it was not the norm, was the ideal—accepted and admired.

In the twenty-first century we live in a world nearly the opposite of that. Christ's church is beleaguered, marginalized and fragmented, so unsure of itself that it has become puny. It whines in a world where it was called to proclaim. Many of our churches are little more than political cells, while others are country clubs for people whose grandfathers were giants of the faith. There *are* growing churches in North America today. Some are very legalistic and literalist, and they provide certainty for people who want a religion of blacks and whites. "God said it. I believe it. End of discussion." Others preach a guilt-free God-loves-everybody-I'm-Okay-You're-Okay religion. Neither of those alternatives will do for most Lutherans. Meanwhile, the Evangelical Lutheran Church in America is shrinking. Maybe your congregation is healthy and growing, but the national church is not.

Our vision is too narrow. The church is shrinking in Europe and North America, but it is growing in Asia, in Africa and in South America. Just today, again, I read in a news magazine a statement by an Indian Christian. Christianity has moved to the Southern Hemisphere: that was his theme.

It is interesting that in Africa, for example, Christians of whatever denomination appear to be better educated in the faith and to stand more firmly on their theological roots than their counterparts in Europe and North America. They are saying to us, "What you are doing does not sound like the faith you brought to us a generation or so ago."

This is no time to hold a funeral for the Christian faith.

Neither is it a time to cling to buildings and synods and organizations here at home that have abandoned Christ, never mind how vital they once were. The Lutheran church may be vigorous in Tanzania, but in the United States it sometimes looks like a wobbly grandfather who can't remember the names of his family members.

It is a time to open our eyes and ears. The United States is still, statistically, one of the most "religious" countries in the developed West. Yet fewer and fewer Americans attend church regularly, tithe, identify with any particular denomination, or let their Christianity affect their decisions. Sixty years ago, almost everyone went to church at least once in awhile. We decried the Christmas-and-Easter crowd, but still, they were there! Today, depending on where you live, 25-40% of Americans attend church at least once a month. In a typical ELCA church, about 30% of the baptized members will attend on any given Sunday. In an informal group of women of which I have been a part for thirty years, I am the only one who attends church regularly; two or three others attend occasionally. In my immediate neighborhood, from nine houses, two families attend church. What was once central to American life, and is still central to mine, is no longer the cultural norm.

We must be realistic. The place of the church in the cultural and political life in the United States is a smaller place than it was fifty years ago. As we abandon our firmly held beliefs, the society loses interest in the voice of the church.

A friend said recently—*says* frequently—"I haven't left the

Lutheran church; it has left me." There are Lutherans who say, "and well it should. The world has changed; the church must change with it. If the church has left you behind, so be it. The church is going where it must if it is to survive." I agree with that in part. Five years ago I often said (and meant it) that I needed a liturgical service and a good choir to anchor my worship. My needs are fewer now. If the word is truly preached, law *and* gospel, if the sacraments of the Lord's Supper and Holy Baptism are rightly administered, well, I can be satisfied. The scripture and Lutheran theology are more important to me than a particular liturgy or a good choir or a Gothic sanctuary.

The church has been changing since St. Paul first set out from Damascus. It takes different forms in different places. Worship patterns, hymns, patterns of education and church organization change. But the church's mission, and therefore its message, stays the same. This, it turns out, is a very Lutheran understanding of the church. The Augsburg Confession (the primary confessional document of Lutheranism) declares that the church comes into being wherever the gospel is purely preached and the sacraments are rightly administered—only that. Whether we sing at all, whether we light candles or decorate our sanctuaries with elegant paraments, these are matters of indifference. Or if you prefer, they are matters of taste. They do not define church or worship. That is classic Lutheran belief.

The One whom we serve, the One who died for us, is the same yesterday and today and forever. We live in a changing world, but we are held together by One Lord. He did not lay out a plan for proper worship. He gave us no "how to" manual for starting and maintaining churches, and He gave us no simple rules to answer every question of life and morals that presents itself. He gave us His Word, and He gave us our reason. He gave us each other and called us His body. In the light of His Word, always in that light, we address the issues of our day. That is not the same as taking the Bible literally, word for word, nor is it an attempt to maintain a church today which is exactly like the First Century church. Neither is it license to ignore the obvious meaning of Biblical texts, to do whatever pleases us, whatever will make us popular, or whatever we can get a majority to affirm.

And that is the rub. The Lutheran church, particularly the Evangelical Lutheran Church in America, is making decisions and acting in ways that many of us fear stand outside the light of God's Word. Where is the light of the Word or the soundness of the reasoning for sex outside marriage, for abortion, for abandoning the doctrine of just war, for sanctioning homosexual behavior, for binding ourselves to a fictional historic episcopate, or for feminizing scripture and our hymns, just to mention a few troubling issues?

Scripture is full of promise for the remnant, the outcast, the weak and the humble. We are promised that if, like Moses, we are poor speakers, God will send an Aaron to speak for us. We are promised that if we are few, He will be with just two or three of us together. We are told that remarkable things can happen. A tent-maker can become the first missionary to the world. A few contentious fishermen can witness even to rabbis and scholars. A slaver can repent and write *Amazing Grace.* A few Norwegians can start a great college, and a group of farmers on the plains can build a white clapboard church with a steeple and two outhouses, working whenever they can get away from the farm chores. The ELCA may depart from the Lutheran faith, but the Christian church will not die, and neither will the Lutheran faith. Lutheran understandings of the priesthood of all believers, grace alone, faith alone and the word alone, and the salvation that is our gift from Jesus Christ from the day of our baptism is our incorruptible treasure. Yet it is possible that in our time we may well be the remnant.

Of course there are still faithful Lutherans in the United States. Of course there are vital and faithful congregations. But it begins to look as if there is a cancer in the body. Those of us who are old enough know that it is possible to live for a very long time while various things go wrong with our bodies. We can limp along with canes and have surgeries to cut out offending parts and repair others. We can take hands-full of pills and get along. But we know it is a losing game. Is the Lutheran church in that situation? There are worrying signs.

How many of us know the basics of the Christian faith? How many of us, even fresh confirmands, can confidently state what justification by faith *alone* means? How can we be Lutheran if we don't know what a Lutheran is? The ELCA and its leaders are not necessarily *Lutheran.* Saying you are Lutheran, pointing to your collar turned backwards to prove it—that is not persuasive. The ELCA is shaky because it is not standing on very firm ground.

Will the current problems go away? Will they be addressed honestly, with faithfulness to the scripture and to our Lutheran heritage? Are there enough men and women of courage to speak out? Are our congregations willing to educate themselves? That remains to be seen. Are we prepared to be a beacon for the faith if it means we must stand in opposition to the culture? Do we know how to love the sinner and still name the sin?

All my life I have heard earnest Christians speak some variation of the notion that when the church is comfortable and acceptable in the society, it grows weak; when it is under siege it grows strong. We are about to find out if that is true.

There are real things wrong with what the ELCA is doing and proposing to do. We can't keep it in the family any more. Even the newspapers chronicle our troubles. Individuals and organizations are springing up to face these challenges, yet many if not most ordinary Lutheran laymen are unaware of the magnitude of them. They do not realize that the church of their fathers really could dissolve in the foreseeable future. Many hope that their congregation will weather the storm intact. They imagine that what the ELCA does nationally need not affect

Our Savior's in Des Moines or St Paul's in Sacramento, or First Lutheran in East Orange.

Some think we can take back the church—that the ELCA can be reformed from within. Perhaps. But it will not happen if we keep our heads down and our mouths shut. The ELCA is only a human framework for the work of the true church on earth. We are not fighting powers and principalities. I keep telling myself that.

Our job, like Brother Cadfael's, is to do the Lord's work as we find it in our path.

Can We Talk?

We have to. It can't just be idle talk. At this very moment, issues of human sexuality, marital definition, the priesthood of all believers, diversity quotas within the church, hymnody, the feminization of scripture and church programs, representation by congregations and individuals in church-wide decision-making—all are on the table and due to be discussed and/or voted on at the Church Wide Assembly in Orlando, Florida, in August, 2005.

There are rules for this kind of talk.

Rules of Engagement

First, we have to **frame the question**. For each discussion, we must first ask: what *exactly* is the issue? If there are several related issues, each one must be stated as clearly and simply as possible and then they must be given priorities. Some questions cannot properly be considered until more basic questions are decided.

The discussions that are taking place on the sexuality-marriage-ordination questions—at least those I have witnessed and participated in—suffered from lack of prioritization and question framing. As a result, the discussions generated considerable heat and very little light.

We must **define the terms** in the well-framed question. How can we talk if we mean different things by the words we use?

In the Lutheran church we must also **separate kingdom-of-heaven discussions** from **kingdom-of-this-world discussions**. We recognize that the law applies both in the spiritual and the civil realm. Both have their place, but they are not necessarily identical. That distinction is a great advantage in church wide decision-making.

We must bring good will, discernment and intelligence to the table, sifting informed and "expert" opinion from the rest. We must recognize that **not all statements, not all "sides" in any discussion of morality have equal value**, for in the church (and in life generally) not everything is relative and not every position is equally valid. We must look to scripture and our Lutheran theology for standards by which to measure the validity of arguments and opinions.

Forewarned, Forearmed

In the main, the issues before the church are coming from the ELCA offices in Chicago, the synod offices, and the ELCA church council and its committees. These issues are not subjects most congregations and lay people are raising. These are issues driven by the few who occupy positions of power and leadership in the ELCA. They are proposing changes in our associations, our governing policies, and our historic mission. They have powerful advantages. They have the staff, the organization, the money, and the publications.

The ELCA leadership has been using some stock arguments in all the issues before the church. A good debater and a good football coach consider it a great advantage to know what plays (or arguments) are going to be used in the game. We are lucky. We have enough history of controversy in the ELCA to know the basic arguments. What's in the official play-book? Here are the big five:

1.The people the ELCA "advocates for" are nice people.

That justifies the proposed action, whatever it is, says this argument. This argument is generously used in advocating for ELCA ordination and rostering of people who are part of the GLBT community. It was used in selling the CCM. (The CCM is the ELCA-ECUSA agreement for "full communion." More about that in "The CCM: Not Your Ordinary Ecumenical Agreement.") When the CCM predecessor, the *Concordat,* failed to pass at the 1997 ELCA Church-wide Assembly, *The Lutheran Magazine* ran a cover picture of a woman in tears because she (a Lutheran) and her husband (an Episcopalian) were not going to be able to worship in one unified Lutheran-Episcopal fellowship. Obviously she was a nice person who cared very much about her family. That was the point.

A problematic point: one nice person's needs and desires may well conflict with anothers. Don't the "nice people" factors cancel each other out?

A pastor recently told me he is willing to consider ordaining homosexuals for the pastorate because he has worked with some wonderful homosexuals in church settings, and yes, they were such nice (and competent) people. The argument is also made for diversity questions, charitable determinations, etc.

In the church that believes we are all saints, all sinners, all the time, what kind of theology is this "nice people" stuff?

2. It is a matter of civil rights.

For Lutherans, this is a *two kingdoms issue.* It has been argued that the very idea of civil rights comes from Christianity, and that Luther's emphasis on the priesthood of all believers further fueled the individualism that, to some extent, underlies our belief in civil rights. Civil rights in the United States are defined by civil law and governmental action. In the civil realm, Lutherans recognize the authority of the government, as Christ taught. The church and its members are called to be good citizens.

We participate in government as Christians, speaking God's Word there as everywhere. We are not the Supreme Court.

On the other hand, we do not defer to the civil realm for our understanding of our moral responsibilities as Christians. We are called, in fact, to do the opposite. We are called to be responsible Christians, living and speaking God's Word in and to the world. Membership in our church is not a *right.* Participation in the church is never a matter of *right.* Salvation is not a *right.* The call to any kind of service in the church is not a *right.* In the church, the rules by which we operate as the body of Christ fall under the authority of God, and we refer primarily to his Word for direction in these matters. We don't ask the government of the land to tell us what is forbidden and what is allowed among us as we function in the church. In the United States, our Constitution guarantees us the right to be a church, to preach the Word as we understand it, and to practice our faith in this society. For that, we are grateful. But it is deceitful for the church to hide behind that civil authority in order to do things that are questionable in the kingdom of God.

As it relates to the culture, the church must speak with the authority of the One whose intentions for culture are central to our faith. We do not blindly follow culture. We participate intentionally (as opposed to accidentally) in making culture when we are true to our calling. That includes Christian participation in government. We do it *as Christians.*

3.We know more than any people in history have ever known; our superiority justifies actions with which our forefathers, in their ignorance, would have disagreed.

Some variation of this argument is behind the revisionist view of scripture. Revisionists claim that scripture doesn't say what we have always thought it says, or that it doesn't apply in today's advanced world. The same argument is sometimes made about Lutheran theology and about some parts of our confessions. There are those in the ELCA who question even the virgin birth and the resurrection of Christ based on the idea that nowadays we know better.

This arrogant confidence, that we in this generation stand at the peak of civilization, is a hallmark of contemporary thought. It is the father of the "dead white guys" view of history, and the "don't trust anyone over thirty" mantra of the sixties generation, as well as the "science tells us" theme song of our age. As a result, we study the past less and less, and the less we know of the history and philosophy of our forefathers the more firmly we can believe in our own superiority, and the more deluded and ignorant we become.

It is interesting to note that, in this advanced society, certain self-identified elite spokesmen believe that, not only is this the wisest and best of all preceding worlds, but they are themselves the few *best* of the best, those *anointed*, in Dr. Thomas Sowell's terminology, to inform and direct the rest of us. (*Vision of the Anointed,* Thomas Sowell, Basic Books, New York, NY, 1995.) The name for this philosophic posture is pride. The price of adhering to that view is the loss of the common sense and home-grown wisdom of ordinary folks, as well as an alienation from a sobering and inspiring past. The church has more than its share of the self-proclaimed *elite*.

4. Christian love demands it.

This is the ace of spades in any modern day religious conflict. A pastor I know recently asked, "How did we get from unconditional love to unconditional acceptance of any and all behaviors?" That is the right question. *Love* in these discussions of church issues is rarely defined, and the term is used variously (sometimes in the same sentence) to mean sexual erotic love or selfless agape love. Much of the time *love* and *acceptance* are used interchangeably. Any parent knows what a trap that is. The better I love my children, the more I want them to be principled, self-disciplined, moral, educated people. Approving of everything they do (spitting on the sidewalk, whacking their siblings, pocketing a candy bar in the grocery store, sassing the teacher) is not helpful. Love is neither easy nor mindlessly all-affirming. Love makes demands because love desires the best for our neighbor.

5. It's going to happen anyway.

This is more a flag of surrender than an argument, but it is used as if it were a valid defense. We are told, in this argument, that "This is the direction society is moving, and we might as well (we had better) get with the program. It is going to happen whether we like it or not, and we surely don't want to be left behind." In a domestic way, that is the mother who decides to pour Junior's milk on the floor right now because he's going to spill it before the meal is over anyway.

Many earnest Lutherans respond by saying, "I'm not ready for this yet." That is the cry of the man who is already down on one knee and getting ready to go down on the other. It is the chorus of those who want to register a weak protest, just in case they have an opportunity some day to say "I told you so". Since when has the church considered it appropriate to give its stamp of approval to whatever scheme or direction or behavior sinful people come up with? Since when do we watch eagerly to see which way the world is running so we can follow it as quickly as possible?

Why Do They Want It?

Just yesterday an acquaintance of mine, a re-oriented homosexual who is an ardent and grateful believer, e-mailed me asking the question, "Why do the bishops want this?" He was speaking of the ordination of non-celibate homosexuals, but he could have been referring to any of several issues. The question is asked. You and I could sit around for days discussing that. *I* don't know what motivates them. *They* may not know. We can only see what they do. And that is enough.

Does it matter? The decisions the ELCA makes in the next year or two will have the same effect whatever the motivations of those who prevail. In 2005, the ELCA Church Wide Assembly is scheduled to vote on whether or not to ordain "practicing" homosexuals, and whether or not to "bless" same sex unions. It is also scheduled to vote on a new worship and hymn book. In 2007, a statement on Christian sexuality is due to be voted on at Church Wide Assembly. All of these votes, plus many less visible issues, will be decided. Because there is no truly representational decision-making in the ELCA, (see "The House with the Orange Door") 99.44% of us (more, really) are mere observers of this process. We may be noisy observers, but we are still just observers.

The hope, however, is that we can make our voices effective. We are way beyond just wanting to be heard. "There, there, it's going to be all right. You'll see," just won't do it anymore. Yes, we'll talk. The more of us the better. But there's no point unless the folks who frame the questions and vote on them pay attention.

I am so Lutheran that I hate it when we speak of any of our pastors and bishops as "they". (It's hard to tell, but I know for sure that *some* bishops and *some* pastors do not deserve to be "they".)

In the Lutheran church, among the priesthood of all believers, it should be *we*. Not identical *we's,* but we the family. We solve the problems of the church. We pray together for wisdom. We determine the direction of this denomination, under God, by the light of scripture, together. We do so remembering Matthew 20:25b-26: "You know that the rulers of the Gentiles lord it over them, and their high officials exercise authority over them. Not so with you. Instead, whoever wants to become great among you must be your servant." (NIV) We do this inside the safety net and secure home of scripture and a cohesive theology. At least we do when we are *Lutheran.*

When our bishops and the staff at ELCA headquarters say "we", do they include you and me and our fellow members in the pews?

The House with the Orange Door

Once upon a time there was a neighborhood that had strict covenants. Anyone who bought or built within that community agreed in writing (it's called a covenant) that his house would be either a white clapboard or a red brick prairie Colonial style, no more than two stories high. All front yards would be bluegrass lawns with at least one tree and no more than three, and the lawns would be mowed during growing season at least weekly. No cars would be allowed on the street between the hours of 2 AM and 6 AM. Back yards would either be fenced or would also be well maintained. A home owners' association was elected yearly, and fees to maintain sidewalks, remove trash and review building permits were established.

Things went along swimmingly for several years. Then one day the family at 2055 Elm in the subdivision painted the front door a vibrant orange. It raised a few eyebrows, but it wasn't in violation of the code, so the home owners' association wisely ignored it. Over the next year or so, the lawn deteriorated. A healthy crop of Canadian thistles appeared in the south lawn, and one of the three maple trees in the front died. No one removed it. The president of the home owners' association made a call on the family. It was all very cordial. But the thistles remained, and the rotting tree. The following summer the family bought a used RV, which they parked in front of the house. It stayed there day and night except for three periods of time when the family went travelling in it. They made no arrangements for lawn mowing while they were away. Again, the home owners' association felt a call was necessary. This time the officers all came. Coffee and chocolate chip cookies were served, promises were made. It was all very amicable. But the RV remained, along with the thistles and the now broken tree. Six months later, a crew arrived one morning and painted the entire exterior of the house purple. That was the very last straw. The HOA board of directors and a delegation of six of the neighbors descended on the house. This time they refused the gin and tonics that were offered, and the guacamole and the blue corn chips. Demands were made. A plan for remedying the situation would be required in two weeks. The HOA would return two weeks from that very evening, to approve (or not) the plans.

The big day arrived. The HOA delegation knocked at the door. As they stood on the porch, the gentleman of the house handed them a typed proposal and suggested that they retire somewhere else to review it and get back to him. The delegation was taken aback, but they regrouped quickly and went to the president's house to look over the proposal.

The proposal promised to build a six foot cedar fence around the back yard and put the RV back there. It promised to reroof the house and install new windows. It promised to plant zinnias in front of the house in the spring, and to paint the door magenta. Signed contracts to do the work were attached to the proposal.

The HOA delegates looked at each other. What about the orange door and the purple paint? What about the weeds? We didn't ask them to do any roofing, and a bed of zinnias, well really! What do you suppose the officers did? What would you do? When you figure it out, some of us will be very interested in your solution.

The ELCA, too, has a covenant of sorts with its congregations. We will be Lutheran, as defined in the Book of Concord. We are the priesthood of all believers. The members of our congregations are the core of the church. We are the church of justification by faith alone, not works. The church organization at the national level exists to protect, preserve and facilitate the work of congregations of just such a church.

Out here in the congregations, we are mostly conservative, both religiously and politically. The leadership is mostly liberal, both religiously and politically. We want as much congregational autonomy as possible. It's more efficient, more personal, more effective. The leadership is constantly chipping away at congregational authority. Most of us think marriage is a one-man and one-woman deal. The leadership apparently disagrees. Few Lutherans are eager to "return to their Catholic roots." Our leaders have been working to do just that for years. Most of us trusting folks think our bishops and pastors (of course) abide by the official policies of the ELCA. Yet ELCA bishops and pastors are violating them flagrantly, and accusing those who object of being divisive. In our congregations, we see quotas as unnecessary problems. The ELCA is going to "educate" us. In our congregations we generally leave Caesar's business to Caesar, and participate in civil government as individuals, not as congregations. Our leaders speak to government as if they had our permission and consent to advocate for us in civil matters.

The ELCA house is becoming an abomination in the neighborhood.

Take a hard honest look at the structure for decision-making and -implementing in the ELCA. Can you, or even you and several hundred of your closest friends, impact that process? How many letters and web-site forms would it take? How many visits with your bishop? Three fourths of us knew little or nothing about the CCM when it was passed, and objected to its provisions when we learnt them, but the CCM is now binding on us all, and rolling inexorably forward. At least three fourths of us, and in some congregations even more, are opposed to any relaxation or change in the traditional Christian sexual standards. The ELCA is about to abandon it, with, or better yet without, a vote of the Church Wide Assembly.

We are finally waking up to the fact that our convictions, desires and expectations in church matters have no legal effect church-wide. The Lutheran beliefs we have learned and loved are being ignored or altered. We have a vote, each of us. For what do we get to vote? In our congregations we elect delegates to our synod assemblies—the number depends on the size of the congregation. That is the first and last vote we have, unless we become delegates. And what do we get with that vote? We get a delegate with one vote at synod assembly, a delegate who is instructed when he gets there that he represents nobody; he must vote his conscience. The delegate is expected neither to know nor to reflect his congregation's majority positions. How he votes cannot be traced, as one might trace the votes of his representative or senator. Moreover, it has actually happened that, when a delegate from a congregation failed to show up at synod assembly, the bishop of that synod simply appointed a replacement on the spot—a replacement not elected by anybody. Some vote! Some voice!

Each synod assembly (there are sixty-five) elects delegates from that synod to Church Wide Assembly. The candidates are nominated and their names are submitted to an elections committee that sifts, selects and organizes them into categories so that the election will produce the required percentages of female and minority delegates. Do you see any opportunity for stacking the house there?

Those delegates elected to Church Wide Assembly, slightly over 1,000, are instructed just as the congregational delegates to synod were—that they are not representatives of anybody but themselves. So they vote on important matters, and what they decide is legally binding on the church. Well, at least for awhile. Between biennial Church Wide Assemblies, the ELCA church council, consisting of 33 delegates from the 65 synods and an advisory non-voting panel of nine bishops, meets twice yearly, and conducts the church's business between Church Wide Assemblies. They can, and sometimes do, reverse the decisions of Church Wide—the 33 of them.

If those bodies faithfully reflected Lutheran confessional positions and the majority views of the laity, it's possible that such a structure could roll along fairly amicably for a long time. But clearly they don't.

Lutherans may be conservative and mostly a-political, but they are not stupid. A lot of us have figured out that, if we don't have the vote, we do have the fuel that runs the car. The ELCA, like all governments, doesn't make money; it only spends it. The ELCA's only sources of income are endowments (when you deed the farm or your house to the ELCA in your will, for example) and the contributions that come from the families in the pews. The money comes from the congregation first to the synod. It is called, interestingly, "benevolence" money. The amount is determined by a combination of constitutional requirement in individual congregational constitutions and by allocation in the churches' annual budgets. The synod then allocates a portion of that money for ELCA operation at the national level. This is a serious business for national. Since we do not have a national church to which all must belong, since membership in the ELCA is entirely voluntary, the church cannot *tax* us. If they tried, those who didn't like the tax could just withdraw from membership. So the ELCA is driven to begging. Not a bad position for Lutherans. Luther's dying words were, "We are all beggars before the Lord, and that's the truth." Moreover, our congregations do not follow a practice of taxing members. Our giving is entirely voluntary, and we like it that way.

It should be easy, then, shouldn't it? Withhold the money.

Here's how that works out in reality. Some members say, "I like what my congregation does. We have to maintain and build property. We want to pay our pastors well and staff the church as well as we can. We like supporting missionaries and we want to do what we can to provide food and clothing for the needy and social services to our members and the community. I am going to pledge $5000 to the church this year. Now don't you give any of this to national. I want to make a statement about my disagreement with national's direction." What a great idea! *Designated giving.* What a naïve idea. Money, whether it is given to the church or to your married kids, is exactly like cups of water in a bucket. Once it goes in, you can't tell my cup of water from the rest of the gallon, and when it gets removed, a cup at a time for whatever purpose, there is no way to know whose water it is and no way to trace where my cup goes. It is *fungible*. (Think how smart you'll sound when you say you understand that money is *fungible.)* So that doesn't work.

"Then," says our frustrated friend, "I'll just not give at all." But his wife says, "We can't do that! What will happen to all the good programs we support through the church? It is our mission to do these things. What about World Hunger, for example?"

So he goes to his church council. "I don't want to quit giving to my church, but I don't want to support homosexual marriage or quota Christianity or bishops who spend my money to tell the president I don't want the U. S. in Iraq or that marriage is not just one-man, one-woman. Can't we agree as a congregation to withhold benevolence from synod—to make the point?" A veritable rumble ensues. It turns out there are a variety of opinions and fears in the congregation, and it's not going to be easy to take such an action, though, for the record, some congregations have done just that.

The simplest and most effective way would be to institute congregational ratification of Church Wide Assembly and ELCA church council resolutions. Congregation by congregation, we would vote yea or nay to the resolutions adopted at Church Wide, and a majority of the congregations would rule.

How likely is that?

So here were are, in front of the orange door to the purple house. The weeds that have grown in our theology are rank and spreading. The church has been painted, to the nation, a color quite out of character with its membership. The abominable used RV of practices borrowed from other places sits snugly in the driveway. We have knocked on this orange door before, and we have reasoned with the inhabitants of the house. We have trusted that they have heard us and that they intend to make changes.

In August 2005, new proposals for church structure and governance have been placed on the table. Their texts are available on the ELCA website. Do they address the issues of congregational autonomy or individual representation in churchwide decision-making? Anything but. They are going to rename and reshuffle the agencies. Maybe the church will follow a new nomination procedure for selecting ELCA church council members. But the purple paint? No. *We here at Higgins Road in Chicago (ELCA headquarters) can be responsive to the membership without changing that. Just look at all the wonderful things we're doing. You don't need to concern yourselves with voting on them.* So they say to us.

When the game is over, we know what people do. Some leave early if the score is so uneven that the outcome is certain. Some hang around to rehash the plays, commiserate with the losers and congratulate the winners. Some carefully go about picking up the pieces and cleaning up the mess. In the end, everybody finally goes home. The lights are turned out. The field is silent.

In the church, some will close their wallets and wait to see what starvation does. Some will preach unity and compromise and lower their standards until the congregation is purged down to the loyalists who know the song "My ELCA Right or Wrong" by heart. Others will write histories and genealogies and hold anniversary celebrations every twenty-five years and invite old members back to help them remember. Some will just hang on till the last pew collapses at the end of the last funeral.

Does it have to be that way? I don't know. There are movements. There are pockets of courage and resolve. So far they have not coalesced into anything with the clout that is necessary. It's not even clear what kind of clout that might be.

We'll See

A Commentary on ELCA Top-Down Management

"We'll see."

Mysterious, imperious, omnipotent. "We'll see." It glides slick and heavy off the parental tongue like an egg dropping into the batter.

"Are we really going to move to Toledo?"

"We'll see."

"Mary Jo got her ears pierced yesterday. When can I get mine done?"

"We'll see."

"Can I have a car in September when I'm sixteen?"

"We'll see."

"We'll see" is a veritable arsenal of linguistic economy. In seven letters, it covers *That's not up to you, We're not going to discuss this now, This is an adult matter, Not now, Wait, Don't ask so many questions.*

It belongs to power. It is regal—it even uses the royal *we.*

When the boss asks if you'll be finished with your financial report in time for Wednesday's staff meeting, "We'll see" will not be an appropriate answer.

When the traffic officer says politely, "May I see your driver's license?" do not reply "We'll see."

And when your bishop says, "We'll see," be very suspicious. But of course he won't actually say, "We'll see." He's too politically savvy. He's been in organizational management too long either to display his muscle in such bad form or to say anything in two words. In the currency of clerical power, he will say "I assure you that that decision has not yet been made." But what he means is, "We'll see."

"Is a bishop the same thing as a synod president?"

"We'll see."

"Are we going to continue teaching Luther's Small Catechism in our churches?"

"We'll see."

"Is Reformation Day still a festival in the Lutheran Church?"

"We'll see."

"If we agree to full communion with the Episcopal Church USA, does that change the role of our pastors?"

"We'll see."

"If a pastor is installed in one of our churches, and he doesn't conform to ELCA policies and Lutheran theology, will he be disciplined?"

"We'll see."

And of course we do see. It is all gradually revealed. We are not invited to participate. Our opinions are not necessarily considered. Like Mom and Dad when we were ten years old, the hierarchy of the church rolls on. It does what it will. We can see the boxes being packed for the move (to Toledo? New Orleans? London? Rome?) but we will have no say in the matter. We'll be asked to pack up our toys too, and get in the truck.

This should not sit well in the church of the priesthood of all believers, of limitless grace for all believers, where we are all beggars at the foot of the cross, even our clergy, and all heirs of salvation, members of God's own family.

What does all this mean for Lutheran congregations? Any kid can tell you.

The CCM: Not Your Ordinary Ecumenical Agreement

The agreement for "full communion" between ELCA Lutherans and the Episcopal Church USA is a parable for Lutherans. It tells us much—more about ourselves than about the ECUSA.

The agreement, Called to Common Mission, (CCM), is the most recent in a series of ecumenical discussions and agreements between the ELCA and its predecessor bodies and several other Christian denominations. Agreements with the Lutheran World Federation, the Moravian Church, the Presbyterian Church USA, the Reformed Church in America and the United Church of Christ have been negotiated during the last fifty years. Each agreement has its own provisions. Generally speaking, these earlier agreements have made inter-denominational cooperations possible without requiring a compromise of Lutheran theology, identity or practice. The CCM is different.

Lutherans have been in discussion with representatives of the ECUSA off and on since 1935. An *Interim Agreement* was formulated in 1982 based on several rounds of discussion involving the LCA, ALC and Association of Evangelical Lutheran Churches. In 1991, two years after the formation of the ELCA, a second document, *The Concordat,* was proposed to the two churches. During its formation there was so much controversy that the ELCA leadership told the 1991 Church Wide Assembly that, should it fail to pass, that would be the end of it. It failed. Nevertheless, *The Concordat* was once again brought before the Church Wide Assembly in 1997, after considerable campaigning in its favor by its authors, bishops and leaders of the ELCA. Again it failed.

What was the rub? One would think that in nearly seventy years of negotiation, no seriously objectionable condition would persist in a proposed document of concord. But it has. The rub is something called the *historic episcopate.* Another term for it is *apostolic succession.* You might guess from the word itself that anything *episcopate* must be central to a church called *Episcopal.* You might also guess from that word's virtual absence in Lutheran theology that it is not central to Lutherans. Right on both counts.

The historic episcopate doomed *The Concordat.*

That was not the fault of the Episcopal Church. The Episcopal Church USA, in all the negotiations and all its public statements, was perfectly transparent about its commitment to the historic episcopate. Never did the ECUSA even hint at the possibility that it would compromise on that. In 1998, in the article *Called to Common Mission and the Episcopate,* Martin Marty said "We have to be clear: any Lutherans, however creative and imaginative or visionary they may be, who say that they propose and desire full communion with Episcopalians but without the episcopate are wasting time, breath, and ink. If they insist on rejecting our reception of the episcopate, they are in effect asking us to end all efforts at 'Agreement' and to go our separate ways, probably permanently."

After the failure of *The Concordat* in 1997, the Presiding Bishop of the ELCA appointed a committee to draft yet another document of agreement. Martin Marty was among the appointees. The bishop charged the committee to draft a document that contained no article opposing the historic episcopate. That's one way to arrive at agreement. Whether Lutherans would concur if they knew about it was not a consideration.

What is this historic episcopate? It is a sacramental system for dispensing grace and ruling the church. It gives bishops (and their priests/pastors) spiritual powers that laity lack. It elevates bishops as special funnels or channels of grace and power. What is the point of the historic episcopate? Its adherents believe that the gospel is only properly passed from one generation to another through such bishops, each one ordained in a sacrament-like ceremony which gives them special powers. This is a firmly held, institution-defining belief of those churches. The Episcopal Church has never agreed to "full communion" with any church that did not agree to the necessity of the historic episcopate, and agree to conform itself to that practice.

ELCA advocates for the CCM call the historic episcopate "a gift."

The idea that grace and the power of the Holy Spirit rest in a few particular people who have been ordained in a particular way — that in itself is the problem for us. Lutheran belief is that faith is generated in each individual by the Holy Spirit working through the Word. Those who insist on the historic episcopate postulate that the Christian faith is "passed down" from one generation to another through persons authorized to do so by an act of ordination. For Lutherans, the *church* is the *body of believers*, all of us, who have received the gift of faith; for Episcopalians, the *church* is the *organization (bishops, priests and deacons in apostolic succession) who guard and promote the faith*. When the ELCA agreed to "accept" the historic episcopate, it agreed that the way we ordain our ministers (pastors) *is* the definition of *church*, for according to the ECUSA, a church is not possible without the historic episcopacy, that is, without that particular channel through which faith comes to lay people. Lutherans believe that justification by faith is what establishes the church—that is, Christ establishes the church, by His saving work. That is what Lutherans are talking about when they say that no one stands between an ordinary person and God.

We can approach God directly. Our forgiveness, and thus our righteousness, comes, not *through* a pastor, priest or bishop, but directly, from God to His people, one on one.

The truth of this great divide between ELCA Lutherans and the Episcopal Church USA is beautifully illustrated by the text of Called to Common Mission itself. Two and a half pages of the official text state the intentions of the two churches to achieve full communion and summarize the common ground the two bodies already share. The remaining seven and a half pages concern themselves with defining the historic episcopate and describing the ways in which the ELCA will conform to and participate in it, stating clearly that full communion between the two bodies will not be realized until the ELCA is completely enfolded in it, a process that will be gradual. Those seven and a half pages are literally peppered with terms such as *episcopate, episcopal collegiality, historic episcopate*, and with references to *oversight, creation of common ministry, implementation of the ordinals, etc.*—all of which refer to what the ELCA will do to come into conformity with the existing ECUSA—an *episcopal* pattern of ministry. Some have said that the document should not be titled Called to Common Mission, but Called to a Common Historic Episcopate. (The text of the CCM is too long to print in this little book. It is available online at ELCA.org and also at ECUSA.org.)

While there is no timeline in the agreement, there are "whens" everywhere in it, making the point that the ELCA *is eventually going to conform to Episcopal practice*, and that "full communion" will not be achieved until that time. We have committed to full communion. So to what do you think, exactly, we have committed?

The church in the fifteenth century had long since decided that some people were official transmitters of the faith. They practiced *episcopal* ministry, that is, they ordained bishops and priests to safeguard the gospel, to interpret it, to make pronouncements about what it requires, to be the keepers, quite literally, of the sacraments and, ultimately, of salvation itself. Moreover, the historic episcopacy distinguishes between its ordained "ministers" in this way: bishops (who received their power in a sacramental ordination) have authority over priests, (on whom they bestow the power of the church) who in turn bestow some powers on deacons. At all three levels, an episcopal clergy brings the gospel to the people. That is the only way it truly comes, according to episcopal thinking. There are thus three *levels* of ministry. (ELCA bishops today will tell you that they are three *expressions* of ministry, but close listening reveals that the three *expressions* operate in a *hierarchy* of authority and discipline. Sounds like *levels* to me.) Bishops in the ECUSA are ordained *again*, first as priests, then as bishops. As they are *ordained* to the "office", they are bishops for life, quite different from the Lutheran pattern of bishops elected for a term. Of course, if you believe that bishops hold the power of the church, it is logical and consistent that they should do so for their lifetime. The power cannot be given and then taken away.

That pattern of church organization led, as we know, to terrible abuses, to a garnering of power in the hands of a few—God's power—as if those few actually could own it.

Are your Lutheran nerves twitching? Lutherans do not believe that *people* either create or transmit faith. The Holy Spirit does that, new, in each one of us. We preach the Word and administer the sacraments, in obedience to God's commands. Our pastors are specially called to do that work.

The church in the fifteenth century, that church solidly grounded in the historic episcopate, had effectively created a distance between "ordinary" people (priests, in Lutheran theology) and God. God's grace seemed far away and difficult to come by. He passed it out to a special few, and the rest—lay people—depended on the crumbs those favored ones passed out. Luther railed against the restrictions of that church, coming even to hate the God that he saw as a remote, demanding, meagerly dispenser of grace. But the day came when he understood the gospel. Finally, reading the Word, he heard the good news—and to him it was terrific good news—that no one stood between him and the God of his salvation; that his salvation depended solely on Christ himself, who offered it freely to anyone who believed. The Word itself, heard and believed, was the vehicle through which grace entered a man's heart and saved him entirely. The Word, not penances meted out by priests.

The church, then, is what happens when God's Word is preached and the sacraments are administered among a group of believers. The faith of those believers is created by the Word. All of us who believe are sinners, made righteous by Christ alone. For Lutherans, the historic episcopate neither defines nor creates *the church.* How could we agree to a document that said otherwise?

It is not obvious that *we* did.

Throughout the process of developing first the Concordat and subsequently Called to Common Mission, the ELCA leadership intentionally and routinely misrepresented the provisions of the documents to the membership of the ELCA. When it was passed at the 1999 Church Wide Assembly, the ELCA was saying it meant different things than the ECUSA was saying. A resolution passed by the Conference of Bishops of the ELCA, called *The Tucson Resolution*, "affirms . . .understandings of 'Called to Common Mission'." That resolution, though the bishops were promised that it would be a part of Called to Common Mission, though it was voted on by the Church Wide Assembly (as an amendment), and though it was printed in the official copies of the CCM text, was declared by Secretary Lowell Almen *not* to be part of the CCM, and the ECUSA was not asked to vote on it. The Episcopal House of Bishops issued its own interpretation of the CCM, which differed markedly from the Tucson Resolution. Just one example:

The *Tucson Resolution* of the ELCA Conference of Bishops states that there is in CCM ". . .*no requirement that the Evan-*

gelical Lutheran Church in America must eventually adopt the three-fold order of ministry. Rather, Called to Common Mission recognizes that the present understanding of one ordained ministry in the Evangelical Lutheran Church in America, including both pastors and bishops may continue in effect." That is, they are saying our pastors will all be ordained in the way they have always been ordained in the Lutheran Church. Nothing will change.

Bishops in the Episcopal church, in their *Mind of the House Resolution* say: "*The Episcopal Church continues to maintain. . .that 'three distinct orders of ordained ministers', namely, bishops, priests, and deacons, are 'characteristic of Christ's holy catholic church,' and that 'it has been, and is, the intention and purpose of this Church to maintain and continue these three orders.* "That is, bishops, priests/pastors, deacons are distinctly separate "orders" of church ministry—separate from lay people because of their ordination, and separate from each other in the kind of power each has. Thus, when the ELCA is in "full communion" with the ECUSA, the ELCA will understand ministry in that way, too, and will conform to episcopal practice.

For the record, the ELCA conference of bishops is not authorized to act in this way. So the bishops made a clarifying pronouncement, which is not, in the Lutheran church, binding. It was voted on and passed at Church Wide Assembly, which would seem to have made it binding. Then an officer of the ELCA (on whose authority?) said to the ECUSA, "Never mind. It isn't binding. You may ignore it." Which they did. What goes on here?

How did *we* in the ELCA adopt the CCM? First, we were given false assurances about the real portent of the CCM document. The ELCA leadership campaigned aggressively among its bishops, pastors and delegates to CWA for its passage, while keeping a very low profile about the CCM in the congregations. It tried its best to control the information concerning CCM that was given to delegates, chiefly by not publishing names of delegates so as to prevent interested parties other than official ELCA agencies from sending them information. Before the 1999 Church Wide Assembly that passed the CCM, at least 20 of the 65 synods of the ELCA went on record as opposing the passage of the CCM. (Not all synods took such votes.) When the CCM came before the Church Wide Assembly, it passed by a margin of 27 votes out of more than a thousand. Who voted? Delegates selected by each synod at their synod assemblies. What is wrong with this picture?

The delegates were told frequently and authoritatively that they did not *represent* their synods or their congregations. They were expected to "vote their conscience." It appears that several delegate consciences were not in agreement with the synods that sent them.

According to Dr. Tim Huffman of Trinity Lutheran Seminary in Columbus, Ohio, 73% of ELCA Lutherans "knew nothing or virtually nothing" about the CCM at the time it was passed. ELCA pastor Neal Snider calculates that those who voted to approve the CCM constitute 0.00014% of the 5,200,000 members of the ELCA, or about 14 out of 100,000.

In the ELCA, that's that. The CCM is a done deal, and gradually its provisions will be fully implemented. While there are movements afoot to amend the CCM (see WordAlone Admonition in *Resources*), so far they have been unsuccessful.

The CCM will effectively turn the ELCA into an Episcopal church. The questions that beg an answer are these: If some Lutheran pastors, laymen, whoever, would be happier in an Episcopalian church, what has prevented them, individually, from joining one? What is lacking in Lutheran understanding of salvation that episcopal succession would satisfy? Why should a body of over five million souls abandon its historic understanding of the church for the forms and very different understandings of a body one third its size? What happens to the priesthood of all believers, to lay presidency at Holy Communion, to the theology of faith alone in Christ's grace alone through the work of the Holy Spirit in the Word alone? Are we still Lutherans?

The ELCA has no provision for affirmation of Church Wide Assembly actions by congregations or even by synods. No congregational votes will ever be taken. ELCA organizational structure does not permit it. Faced with that reality, the only remedy, if we want to be Lutheran, is to leave the ELCA.

The Good, the Bad and the Ugly: Sex and the Church

At the Church Wide Assembly in August 2005, the ELCA will be asked to vote on whether to allow ordination of non-celibate gay clergy and whether to approve, or "bless", same-gender "unions". It may vote to accept or to reject both, or just one, or it may vote to table the whole thing for the time being. And, who knows? some other "solution" to the "problem" may be proposed.

What is it about the whole homosexual issue that so riles the church? The society at large, too? For the church, and for the society, the homosexual issue calls into question not just some long-held standards for behavior, but the very foundations on which we have built a culture. The laws, taboos, expectations, games, medical practice, social welfare, the way we raise children and educate them, our entertainments, even our own marriages are all called into question. In the church, our very existence is challenged. Ordinary folk of a certain age say "No, no, no" and refuse to get too close. They don't want to talk about any homosexual issue. They shut it out in the vain hope that it's not as bad as they fear, that it will resolve itself. We can be loving, can't we? We can be accepting. After all, we've seen it all in the church. We have drug and alcohol rehab programs and adoption agencies and programs to care for children after school till their parents get home from work. We know what the world is like. We can do this, too. Can't we? Young people in the church, subjected to a barrage of material at school and in the media and at ELCA youth gatherings, often say it's no big deal. We can live with it.

Maybe, maybe not. We haven't made a very good beginning.

After one of the sessions our congregation held using *Journeying Together Faithfully II,* the ELCA's study on the questions of celibate clergy and the blessing of same-sex "unions," one of my fellow members said to me "You know, we're too shy about the whole matter of sex. We need to talk about this." I am not known in the congregation for reticence, but that shut me up! Is there anything more talked about, hinted at, displayed, strutted in the malls and sweated on the screen than sex? Of course she's right in a way—not the way she thought. Much that is sexual in public has become so common that we don't talk about it. Things have changed a lot in fifty years. Sexual terms and epithets are everywhere. Youth and young adulthood is pictured as a time of more or less constant rutting. Sex is so omnipresent and the standards of what is private and what is intimate have fallen so low that homosexuals who want to get our attention are driven to parade nearly naked, costumed and tattooed and acting out sexual intercourse, on Pennsylvania Avenue in Washington, D. C. As the standard of decency falls the threshold for shock rises. Movies complete with graphic scenes of sexual intercourse play in every small town and on HBO daily. It's more and more difficult to give a child a long, gentle, leisurely and innocent childhood, and fewer people try. Talk about it indeed!

My friend was right, though. We do need to talk about it. *All* about it. As we continued in the *Journeying Together Faithfully Study,* one glaring omission became obvious. We were not going to talk about "what they do" or about the consequences, physical, emotional, or spiritual, of what they do.

I visited friends in another city a short time ago. At one point in the conversation, my host said, "I know gays are nice guys." Come on. Can you say that *categorically* about any group? "I know Croatians are nice guys." "I know Chicanos are nice guys." "I know Catholics are nice guys." "I know engineers are nice guys." "I know people from Ames, Iowa are nice guys." As a Christian can you say that about anybody? "I know pastors are nice guys." We humans are not, categorically, "nice guys."

Your dinner guests leave, you close the door behind them, and arm-in-arm go to the kitchen to clean up the mess. "Wasn't that a good evening?" you say to one another. "Good conversation. I really like ______. What a nice guy." And you mean it. And on a certain level it's true. And then you undress for bed, brush your teeth, turn out the light, and say your evening prayer. "Deliver us from evil. What evil have I done today? What obligation has gone undone? I am indeed a sinner yet, and once more I come to You, with my sorrows and regrets and good intentions, and beg of You that boundless grace, still, in which I live a saint."

Am I a nice guy? This dear man beside me, is he a nice guy? Maybe. In a limited way. But there is no hiding the fact that I and he and our guests and all those Croatians and Chicanos and Catholics and engineers and people from Ames, Iowa are imperfect in all the ways that make the world and our families what they are. Gays, too. No one is perfect. No, not one.

So let's get over the talk about what nice people homosexuals are. I am suspicious when anyone is too effusively praised. Every single man knows all about the girl with the great personality. Several of us females have also met Karen's brother who is a really swell guy who just hasn't found the right girl yet. Why, I want to know, are our church leaders so anxious to tell us what great committed relationships these homosexual couples have, and how loving they are? Is that what you say about your married friends? Is that how we commend ourselves to one another? If we are married, in my circles anyway, the commitment is *assumed*, and the *loving* is understood to be a mystery to those outside the marriage. We see glimpses of it.

It's *their* marriage. Glimpses are enough for us.

There is a reason why the church, so eager to ordain "practicing homosexuals" and "bless" same-sex "unions," is both effusive and apparently naïve in its descriptions of homosexuals and so unwilling to be specific about their lives. The ELCA is going to ask the Church Wide Assembly to vote on these two issues in 2005. The ELCA has meanwhile *been* ordaining and installing non-celibate pastors regularly, sometimes with no disciplinary action from the bishops, sometimes with discipline exercised and later removed while the unrepentant pastor remains in place. Individual pastors have performed hundreds of "same-sex blessings"—again, without sanction. The proposed hymnal, which will also be voted on in 2005, even has marriage settings "suitable" for such ceremonies. All of this is going on, and the church has not, to date, convened a theological and Biblical forum to examine questions such as: "Is homosexuality the intention of our Lord? What does the Bible actually say about it? What do we know by the tests of its 'fruits'? Is it sin?" Do the "higher-ups" at the ELCA think we don't notice, that we don't know *anything*? The ELCA is in a bad spot. It cannot discuss "what they do" without implicating itself in actions it is tacitly approving already.

One of the difficulties of the *Journeying Together Faithfully Study* is that it is impossible to discuss the issues of homosexual ordinations or same-sex unions without asking the foundational questions. Most of what is discussed scratches at the issue of homosexual behavior itself. We can't help it. We need to know about homosexual behavior and its consequences in order to make a decision. Perhaps it is more nearly correct to say we need information to defend our decision to each other and to the world. We need to think about the morality of the behaviors in relation to the issues we will be voting on. But there is no framework for such a discussion presented in the material, and no evidence to examine.

For our purposes from here on, the term *homosexual* will

refer to persons who engage in homosexual acts. People who consider themselves homosexual or have homosexual tendencies but live celibate lives do not figure either in the consideration of whether the behavior is sinful or in the questions before the church. Homosexuality is, in the opinion of many thoughtful Christians and some others, not a *condition* but a behavior. It is apparently often an *un*chosen inclination, but if it is not acted out, if the individual has made a celibate peace with it, as in all pastoral counseling situations, it is none of our business unless the individual asks for help.

How many homosexuals are there? In the largest cities, the percentage is around ten percent in the U. S. In rural areas it is one percent or less. Across the nation as a whole, the figures range between 2.5% and 3.0%. In Europe the numbers are a little smaller across the continent. That figure undoubtedly varies by country. The percent of adolescent males who now consider themselves homosexual is growing. Many public schools now teach that homosexuality is an acceptable option. Some school districts even mandate such teaching. Boys under the age of fourteen are most vulnerable because in their formative years, it is common for boys to be somewhat ambivalent about their sexual identification. Girls can identify for life with their mothers, the primary care-givers and nurturers, but boys must separate emotionally from their mothers and identify with their fathers. Of course the whole picture is more complex than that, but that is the essence of it. Parents and the church have an obligation to intervene when they observe distorted sexual identity patterns developing in a boy. *Gender Identity Dysfunction*, as it is called, can be successfully treated in a young child. Untreated, 75% of boys with GID will become homosexuals.[1] In the absence of a father, or as an additional male model, pastors and church youth leaders can help boys effectively maneuver through that difficult time.

Many homosexuals find male friendships outside of sexual activities difficult. Joe Dallas, an ex-gay, now director of Genesis Counseling in Orange, California talks about how important it was for him to learn to develop non-sexual male friendships in his healing process.[2] It is important in developing a strong gender identity, especially for a boy, to have a loving non-sexual relationship with his father or some male who is a constant presence in his life.

Is it genetic? Not that anyone has been able to discover. The one study that seemed most likely to have identified a "gay gene" was done by Dean Hamer in 1993, and the news media jumped on it with fervor. On closer reading , it did *not* establish a specific "gay" marker. Dr. Hamer, who is gay himself, when asked if homosexuality was rooted solely in biology, replied, "Absolutely not. From twins studies we already know that half or more of the variability in sexual orientation is not inherited."[3] In recent years the search for a genetic marker has waned or disappeared. "Andrew Sullivan, gay activist and author says. . .it would be self-deception to think of homosexuality as genetically inherited."[4] Ruth Hubbard, professor emeritus at Harvard University and board member of the Council for Responsible Genetics, has this to say: "Searching for the 'gay gene' is not even a worthwhile pursuit. I don't think there is any single gene that governs complex human behavior. There are genetic components in everything we do. It is foolish to say genes are not involved, but I don't think they are decisive."[5] ELCA pastors and speakers on this issue routinely assert that homosexuality is genetic. It's time they stopped that.

Is it a choice? Not usually. Not in the ways we are accustomed to think of choice. Half of all boys who are sexually molested by a homosexual before they are fourteen will themselves become homosexuals. Early victimization is one of the identifiable factors. Preoccupation with erotic and pornographic materials in the formative years and beyond is another. A distant same-sex parent or an overly "close" opposite-sex parent is another. Much material has been written on this subject. In the church we should be encouraging research in this area and in the areas of prevention and reorientation. Christian compassion for these our brothers, sisters, nieces, nephews, sons and daughters demands it. A psychiatrist of our acquaintance who works with families emphasizes the importance of intervention with children who exhibit tendencies of identification with their opposite sex. When it is identified and redirected, virtually all such children develop healthy sexual identification.

Is homosexuality pedophilia? The question is in part a matter of legal definition. The answer varies somewhat from state to state in the U. S., and from country to country in Europe. In Holland, the age of demarcation is twelve. Richard John Neuhaus, editor of *First Things* journal, himself a Roman Catholic priest, a convert from Lutheranism, reported in March, 2003 that at that time 4,268 victims of the sexual scandals among the Roman Catholic priesthood had been identified by the *New York Times*, 80% of whom were boys, mainly teenagers.[6] By the year 2000, the Center for Disease Control in Atlanta recorded over 15,000 boys with diseases related to sex with adult males. In the ELCA in 2004 Gerald Patrick Thomas, formerly an ELCA pastor, was convicted of molesting over a dozen boys, mostly teenagers, while serving in three ELCA parish settings: he was sentenced to 397 years in Texas State prison. A jury awarded the victims $37 million: a total pay-out of $69 million was made in this and two other related suits involving Thomas's actions. Was that pedophilia?

The connection between male homosexuals and boys has an ancient history. It was well known in ancient Greece and Rome. In the United States there is an organization, The Man-Boy Love Society, which actively promotes man-boy sex and argues that it is not harmful to the child. Pedophilia is its own "branch" of sexual deviancy, but the frequency of man-boy homosexual activity raises questions about the extent to which homosexual acts with children are pedophilia. We should be asking whether persons who engage in homosexual behavior should be serving in occupations and services that involve the care, nurturing and education of children and teenagers.

What about "committed" homosexual couples? In one study, 28% of homosexual males claimed 1,000 or more lifetime partners. 75% claimed that more than half of their partners were strangers. In general, homosexual relationships seldom last more than two years. A German study of 900 homosexual men who identified themselves as living in "steady relationships" revealed that 83% of those steady partners had frequent homosexual encounters outside the partnership, averaging 115 outside contacts. Another study, done by two homosexuals, involved 156 male couples of whom only 7 maintained fidelity for the period studied.[7]

Homosexual men, depending on the study you read, live to an average age of between 43 and 55. I've seen so many figures that I question the way they are gathered, but in every case, the life expectancy of the average homosexual is placed as at least 20 years less than that of the average American male. That doesn't mean you don't know a few old homosexuals: the statistics also reflect the number of very young deaths.

Why do they die so young? In an article in *First Things,* February 2004, Mary Eberstadt, research fellow at the Hoover Institution, documents that homosexuals suffer in disproportionate numbers from chemical addictions, abuse of alcohol and of licit and illicit drugs. Gay men are, of all groups, most at risk of becoming alcoholic. The *Journal of Gay and Lesbian Psychotherapy* (yes, Virginia, there is one) devoted an entire issue to the subject of gay and lesbian addictions recently. The levels of depression are substantially higher in the gay community, whether the individuals are HIV positive or HIV negative, than they are in general population samples. Suicide and suicide attempts are also higher among homosexuals: 18% of white homosexual males, *vs.* 3% of white males in the general population. These figures come from homosexual sources. Ms. Eberstadt quotes the founders of the Harvey Milk School for gay teenagers in New York City, who claim that nearly one third of all gay teens drop out of school every year, three times the national average.[8]

Homosexuals are famously vulnerable to HIV and related viral killers such as AIDS. That is not the whole story of early death by disease among homosexuals. A whole family of diseases caused by ruptures in the anus and bowel, which provide an entry for feces into the blood-stream, cause several kinds of infections and diseases, many of which are lumped together in the medical literature under the name Gay Bowel Syndrome. In the U. S. we know that most HIV and AIDS victims are male homosexuals. In Africa women are nearly as often (sometimes more) affected. There is reason to believe that the cause is anal intercourse, even with women, which causes the same types of diseases.

Should homosexuals be allowed to adopt and/or have children by artificial and other non-sexual means? That is, again, a question for the legislative and legal systems, but the church as a vehicle for God's voice in the society has a huge stake in the answer. As Mary Eberstadt and others have pointed out, we are now seeing many studies and books that document the great superiority of intact one-father one-mother marriages over any other social structure for raising children. Children in any other setting exhibit greater frequency of all kinds of behavioral, educational, economic, psychological and criminal problems, not to mention the tendency to repeat these unsuccessful patterns in their own family and child-rearing patterns later. We still read articles, especially in the women's magazines, that tell women their children are better off in day care and pre-school, that divorce doesn't hurt children, that "non-traditional" families are lovely, but another voice is now finally being heard. We do read, almost daily, of yet another child who has been injured by a live-in boyfriend in our small northern Colorado town. Teachers of young children tell story after story of the problems children in situations other than the traditional intact family have. Children deserve a home with Dad and Mom.

While we deal lovingly with single-parent families, "blended" families, etc., we should do everything we can to encourage the formation, health and continuance of traditional families. Is a male homosexual a proper model for little boys trying to learn how to be men? Is a lesbian mother a healthy model for daughters? What about for sons? These are legitimate questions and responsible honest people need to ask them. Christians need to ask them.

Data about homosexuality and its societal effects have been so effectively suppressed in the national press and elsewhere that many folks do not believe them. You may say to yourselves, "It's just right wing conservative politics," or "These are just conservative fundamental Christian claims." I invite you to check out the resource list in the back of this book and any website that you can find. There are books and magazines, even in the gay community, which document all these claims. Just last month, an article about a lesbian health fair in California which appeared in our local paper claimed that lesbians are also at higher-than-average risk for certain diseases. Keep your eyes open. There is information even in the most liberal, gay-permeated publications that tells the story. Not in ELCA materials, unfortunately.

Are homosexuals bad people? Not necessarily. No more, certainly than they are all "nice guys." Are they victims? Sometimes, particularly if they are young. What do they have to do with the church? They are fellow Christians, some of them. Some are seekers, as many of us once were. Many are suffering, and not just from diseases. Many are angry, arrogant, activist and in-your-face, and they plan to stay there. Are we commanded to love them, too? The story of the Good Samaritan answers that question. They are our neighbors.

It would be interesting to know what percentage of homosexuals in America are in churches, and how many would like to be but feel unwelcome. I have found no data on those questions. Nor is there any data that I have found which suggests how many at any given time question the lives they lead, and wonder if there is another way.

Within the church, a movement called "Communities of Grace" welcomes homosexuals to affiliated churches where acceptance, counseling and encouragement for healing are offered. Homosexual activists in the ELCA and elsewhere oppose such missions. This summer a group of formerly homosexual people set up a booth at the convention of the National Education Association. Television and newspaper coverage showed how they were attacked verbally, and their materials and booth were shoved and tossed about by homosexuals who objected to their presence.

The ELCA currently has a policy on sexuality and on the relevant requirements for pastors, part of what is creatively called "Visions and Expectations" for *rostered* persons in the ELCA. *Rostered,* in church lingo, means people who are ordained or certified to act as pastors, lay ministers and so on. They are employees, if you will, who have professional status in the church, whom the church *certifies* to possess the character, training and education the ELCA requires of people who, we believe, have an authentic *call* to these vocations. Currently the ELCA states in *Visions and Expectations* that, "It is the policy of the ELCA that all single rostered people, including those who understand themselves to be homosexual, are expected to abstain from sexual relationships." The ELCA Task Force on Human Sexuality has been charged with the responsibility to word a resolution for the Church Wide Assembly (CWA) in August of 2005 which will in some way provide a referendum on the possible ordination of "practicing homosexuals" and the possible "blessing of same-sex unions". We are discussing the issue (or not, as the case may be) without knowing just what the resolution is. Why is the ELCA so late laying the actual resolution on the table?

Two things must be made clear about this discussion in the church. First, we don't know exactly what CWA resolutions we're talking about, and we won't until the resolution comes out of the Task Force. That's a distinct disadvantage. Until we know exactly what the wording of the resolutions is, we are shooting in the dark (as well as off at the mouth.) And second, the issue of whether homosexual acts are, in themselves, sinful from the church's theological and biblical perspective is apparently up for debate. Once again, the church is not saying forthrightly where it stands and documenting it. The ELCA study is full of "some people say" and "other people say." In the Lutheran church, of all places, the church that is heir to a great deal of good sense from Dr. Luther himself about how scripture should be read and weighed, we are reduced to "some people say"! Are we going to vote on that too—whether scripture actually says what it says and whether we have to heed or can safely ignore it?

When the adult Sunday school class at my church began holding discussions prior to the 1993 ELCA statement on human sexuality, two of us who were sitting together in the class turned to each other and said, almost in unison, "What are we doing discussing sex outside of marriage or non-heterosexual sex? That's not up for debate!" The traditional and conservative among us are inclined to say that that issue was decided long ago. That the society was questioning it, well, what else is new? Unfortunately the church, as well as the society, is being challenged aggressively on these issues, so, like it or not, we have to respond. In a battle for your life, you bring out the big guns. (The ELCA has become a pacifist organization lately, so they won't like the metaphor. Oh well.) Inside the church, among the body of Christ, the big gun in the armory is the Word. I suppose we could pray to God to send a hail of fire down on somebody, if only we could decide for sure who, but I have no faith in the success of that kind of prayer.

Inside the church, what the Word tells us is important. *Outside* the church, in addressing the federal marriage amendment, for example, nobody cares what the Bible says about it. That will not be the issue and we should quit trying to make it the issue. There are good reasons to question any societal action that encourages or supports homosexual life styles; in that context the church is but one institutional voice. Christians within the society ought to participate, as savvy informed citizens, but not as tiresome spouters of Bible verses.

Inside the church, and as Christians relating to the secular society, how do we use scripture in situations like this? Lutherans understand that scripture contains both law and gospel, that is, there is law in scripture and we make law to restrain the evil in mankind since the fall. (We'll talk more about uses of the law in the section *What Do Lutherans Believe?*) And there is gospel, *good news.* In the church, we understand the restraining purpose of the law, and we respond in obedience to God's command in Romans 13:10: "Love does no harm to its neighbor. Therefore love is the fulfillment of the law." (NIV) We must ask, then: What are the consequences of homosexual acts? What are the likely consequences to individuals and the society if our church sanctions and/or approves homosexual behavior? At the same time, we must remember the gospel. God forgives repentant sinners. Homosexual acts are forgiveable.

So, finally, what does the Bible say about homosexuality? To begin with, it says absolutely nothing positive about it. Not anywhere. That should give us a clue.

It is interesting that the standard for Christian behavior from early times was sexual chastity. In a letter sent to several of the young churches, the new Christians were advised: "It seemed good to the Holy Spirit and to us not to burden you with anything beyond the following requirements. You are to abstain from food sacrificed to idols, from blood, from the meat of strangled animals and from sexual immorality. You will do well to avoid these things." (Acts 15: 28-29 – NIV). For our day, perhaps we could reword it to say that we are to have nothing to do with false gods such as money, power, Buddhism, and their practices, and to refrain from sexual immorality. Be faithful to the one God and faithful to each other. When the early church fathers tried to simplify the faith for new Christians, sexual morality was one of the two standards of behavior laid down. The fact is that sexual morality is basic to Christian behavior. An early Roman wrote a letter which survives. In it he states that there are some people in his community who live pure lives, worship the one God, and are faithful to their wives. "They are called Christians," he goes on to say, "and I am one of them." Again, the theme. It is significant that he mentions his faithfulness to his wife. In a culture where that was the norm, he would not have bothered.

The first texts most often cited in relation to sexual behavior are the Genesis creation texts. *"Then God said, 'Let us make man in our image, in our likeness."* (Gen. 1:26 – NIV) and then, *"So God created man in his own image, in the image of God he created him; male and female he created them."* (Gen. 1:27 – NIV). That is followed immediately by the injunction to be fruitful and multiply, as well as to subdue and rule over the earth. We can see from these texts that God's image has two faces, male and female, and that one of the chief purposes of mankind is to produce children; the ability to do so is built into creation. It is biological. We are made that way. And the purpose of sex is procreation.

Some people think that is a limited and degrading definition of sex, because sex has also to do with loving and bonding and romance and all that. Consider this: the purpose of food is to sustain the physical body. But we think it's a poor thing to eat "like animals" taking no notice of what we are eating. A whole culture, whole industries have grown up around food and its pleasures. The main purpose of food, or sex, does not rule out its auxiliary pleasures. Consider, too, that the desire for one another lives, in our long lives, well past the possibility of procreation, but in a faithful marriage sex among the elderly is not forbidden. There is no taboo on it. Only the young think it's disgusting.

As for food, we do not, in Christian cultures, stop feeding people who are in the last stages of obviously terminal illness. We can eat, we can engage in sexual intercourse, as long as we live, and in that context, we are acting out the wholeness of God. While we are made in his image, we are made in two kinds, both in his image, and when the two unite, there is a sense in which they are, in their uniting, participating in the completeness, the fullness of God's image. In Genesis 2:20-24, we have the more personal story of the creation of Adam and Eve, and Adam's beautiful praise of the wife God made for him: "This is now bone of my bone, and flesh of my flesh." Robert Gagnon comments on this text: "Marriage is pictured as a *reconstitution* of the two constituent parts. . . .Accordingly, the most essential requirement of human sexual relations—the only one that restores the original sexual unity—is that there be a male and a female to effect this *re*-union."[9] As soon as we know what sexual intercourse is, we can see how the parts fit. Only the union of a man and a woman can produce a child. It's a point to ponder when the question of genetic sexual orientation arises. If it were genetic, the result of some mutation, if it were the unavoidable and consistent behavior of the person(s) in question, homosexuality would die out in a generation. We see in creation what God's intentions are in this regard. St. Paul also makes the point that what is natural, what is intended for human sexual intercourse, is obvious.

Healthy mature sexual love is love for the "other." It is completion, fulfillment, complementarity in the union of the two: male and female. As with so much in creation, there is an aspect of challenge and spiritual growth built in. Marriage requires stretching, reaching out to one's human opposite, body and soul, adapting to and creatively loving our "other." In the context of God's creative intentions, how pale and contorted same-sex romance appears.

Then there are the famous stories of Ham and his father

Noah (Genesis 9) and of Sodom and Gomorrah, (Genesis 19). Ham apparently raped his father Noah. It's not crystal clear to me, for the story only tells us that he "looked on his father's nakedness." His brothers, when they heard (from Ham) that their father was lying naked in his tent, covered him with a blanket without looking at him, apparently the proper thing to do. But Noah, when he awoke, knew what "had been done" to him, which suggests the incestuous homosexual rape. Two wrongs here: incest and male-male sex.

In Sodom and Gomorrah again there is more than one thing wrong with the sex that is proposed. There is certainly a lack of hospitality on the part of those men in the town. It's no way to treat guests, to demand mob sex from them. And worse yet, to demand homosexual sex. The writer of the Ham and Noah story is the same as the writer of the Sodom and Gomorrah story. Both stories illustrate the sexual depravity of that world, and both are emphasizing the depravity of the society. It is not just a little bit immoral. It is horribly so. Same-sex intercourse compounds the evil, greatly, apparently.

The culture of the lands into which the Israelites came was a horrible culture from the standpoint of its sexuality. Bel, Baal, Astarte, later Aprodite, the Egyptian Isis were all gods of "fertility" religions (among other attributes). The Baal religions included sexual initiation rites and temple prostitution, as well as child sacrifice and castration rites. The covenant between Yahweh (the Israelite way of referring to the one God) and the nomadic people who became the nation of Israel emphasized sexual fidelity and a high standard of morality in sexual matters. Throughout the Old Testament, the necessity to be physically and culturally separate from the Baal worshipers is emphasized. It is consistent with St. Paul's summary: we must not engage in or approve behaviors that are harmful to the individual or to the society. Those early cultures were permeated with sexual sickness and the people suffered greatly from it. Such religions flourished into the days of Jesus and beyond, even into the first centuries of the Christian era.

Leviticus is a compendium of shoulds and should nots, practical and spiritual rules for living. It has been called the "holiness code." Much of it is problematic today. The chapters on animal sacrifice, how it is performed and for what offenses, Christians understand to have been superseded by the sacrifice of Christ on the cross. However, the sexual restrictions, all of Chapter 19, have traditionally been held still to apply, because they are invoked by St. Paul, who knew very well that Christ had made a full sacrifice for our sins. Even people who have never heard of the holiness code find the sanctions familiar. We are all naturally repelled by the notion of sex between family members, as well as sex between people of the same sex. We have to suppress that natural aversion in order to commit such acts. Further, in Verses 24 to 30, it is made clear that sexual sins such as these were "how the nations . . .before you" defiled the land. Again, it is the *results* of those behaviors that demonstrate their sinfulness. St. Paul and other first century Christians were well aware of the cult of Aphrodite among the Greeks, and they had to warn against it. Love does no harm to its neighbor.

Romans 1:24-32 and I Corinthians 6:9 are the two texts in the New Testament that specifically deal with homosexuality. In both texts, those who commit these sexual sins are doing so in rejection of God. Paul's particular judgment of the acts is that they are *unnatural*, as he says in Romans 1:20, NIV. ". . .since the creation of the world God's invisible qualities—his eternal power and divine nature—have been clearly seen, being understood from what has been made, so that men are without excuse." We can see how we are made. Our sexual function is stamped in our bodies, male and female. Only by rejecting the Creator, and the Creator's obvious intentions, do men commit such (homosexual) acts, exchanging ". . .natural relations for unnatural ones." (Romans 1:26 – NIV) These texts make it clear also that people who engage in such behaviors encourage others to do so as well, compounding the sin.

In faithfulness to the Bible's clear intentions for our sexual behavior, Christian missionaries throughout the world have preached monogamy and male-female sex *only*. Today Christians outside Europe and North America are appalled at our flagrant violation of the very precepts we brought to them.

Until recently, the Biblical texts, these standards for sexual behavior, were not questioned. They were assumed. Matters which are assumed in any culture are rarely spoken of, and we see throughout scripture that that is the case here. When we consider all taboo subjects, it is obvious that none are much spoken of. They are unthinkable. Unspeakable.

The male-female pairing is *assumed*, both in the Old Testament, and by Christ. Scriptural revisionists in our time say that, because it is so rarely spoken of, undoubtedly Paul and the others didn't know anything about "committed homosexual unions". Obviously Paul knew about homosexuality. Whether committed or not is irrelevant. Is doing something abominable with the same person over and over better than doing it with several? If an act is sinful, isn't it even worse to be committed to it, and to commit another person to it as well?

The revisionists say that it is about the supremacy of love and faithfulness, not the sinfulness of the particular sexual act. Several assumptions underlie that assertion. One, that love and sex (of any kind) are synonymous, and two, that faithfulness is only relevant to sexual relationships. Neither is true. We know many kinds of love if we are lucky—parental love, the love of friends for one another, and love for Our Lord—to name a few. Faithfulness, too, is honored among soldiers, bill-payers, friends, workers and yes, wives and husbands. And it appears that they further assume that love *can* do no harm, a twist on the command that it *should* do no harm. Love, too, is measurable—by its effects.

The revisionist interpreters make much of loneliness in the creation story: "It is not good for man to be alone", claiming that for a homosexual, the only antidote for loneliness is a homosexual partner (or several homosexual partners). Again, it is a straw man. Human companionship is the answer to loneliness. There is no requirement that it be a sexual partner.

Good church people are being told that, if we love at all, as in "Love thy neighbor as thyself," we have to acknowledge homosexual love, too, and we must love the homosexual. It's true, we must love the homosexual, but love, Christian and responsible love, is not *approval.* I love my babies with a love that is unfathomable, but I sure don't love everything they do. We love with the love that sees in each person one whom God created, for whom He has holiness in mind. Christian love is not synonymous with Christ's approval, or the church's either. We love in such a way that we discourage what is evil and encourage what is good in each other. We don't do that perfectly, but that's what we are supposed to do—not place a churchly stamp of approval on anything and everything that Christians and others are moved to do.

Perhaps the worst thing revisionist Bible interpreters do is give in. Some of them admit that scripture forbids homosexual acts and in the strongest way, but they insist that it doesn't apply. (A little like saying defiantly, "We don't care!") We should not be surprised at that. When I taught high school years ago and the kids discussed casually their hopes to marry soon, I told them that they ought to wait till they had gone to college or worked a little while, just to mature a bit. I told them what I had been taught and what I saw—that marriages between teenagers didn't have a very good success rate. They told me that they knew better. They were more mature than their parents at their age, etc. We live in a society that has thought more or less the same thing for two hundred years, that it knows better.

Besides the obvious scriptural texts, those cited above, the Bible is full of stories of men and women, moral and immoral, and in the entire set of sixty-six books, no same-sex "union" is presented for our approval. Family life at its best and worst are portrayed throughout. Abraham and Sarah, Jacob and Rachel, Solomon and Bathsheba, Samson and Delilah, Hannah and Elkanah, Mary and Joseph, Hosea and his unfaithful wife—the heterosexual pattern is obvious, natural and assumed. The wisdom we look for in scripture is consistent in matters of sex.

The Bible is clear on this.

In this twenty-first century, as in Rome at the time of St. Paul, homosexuality is a fact of life. Homosexuals are our friends and neighbors, as well as anonymous people everywhere. Inside the church, we have to decide how we are to deal with people who identify themselves as homosexual. Homosexuality is sinful. It takes a powerful amount of imagination and a perversity of scriptural interpretation (or tossing out of scripture) to claim otherwise. It takes a great blindness to the effects of homosexual behavior as well. But so are gossip, slander, thievery, adultery, murder, envy—all sinful behavior. In the church—God's hospital for sinners, in the popular phrase—we acknowledge that we are, all of us, sinners. Some of our sins may seem worse than others, but on the grand scale, probably there is little difference. Except for sexual sins, which are singled out repeatedly for special attention. Homosexuality is sometimes seen as one sin among many. Let's keep it in that context for a minute.

One of the most poignant and subversive arguments for the acceptance of homosexuality comes from family members who say, "How would you feel if your son or daughter were homosexual? These are our children. How can you relegate them to second-class positions among Christians?" On the strength of that heart-wrenching plea, we in the ELCA are being asked to ordain homosexuals for pastoral positions, and to "bless" their "marital unions."

Let's substitute any one of the other named big sins in that argument. "How would you feel if your son or daughter were a murderer, an embezzler, a thief?" We would not strike out the commandments on that account, would we? We would not set up special ceremonies to approve and "bless" their murder, embezzling and thievery. We would be careful what positions we gave any of them in the church, not because we are unloving, but because we are responsible and prudent. You don't hire a convicted embezzler to manage the church funds. You would not ask the biggest gossip in the church to head the prayer chain, would you? To build our new educational wing, we would not hire a contractor who had just been sued for shoddy workmanship. Likewise, because among other things we should require from our pastors proper modeling of unconfused sexual identity, we should not put homosexuals in pastoral positions. Many churches nowadays require background checks of all persons who deal with children in the church, for example. If a background check identified homosexual activity, would your church consider that person for a youth leader? The idiocy of fawning after homosexuals for pastors, as representatives of the great "diversity" of mankind, should be beyond the imagination of churches. Mankind is particularly diverse in the many ways he can think of to do evil—nothing to celebrate.

Inside the church, specifically here inside the ELCA, it should not be a question. But in the ELCA, we have a powerful faction in leadership positions that is committed both to ordaining homosexuals and to blessing same-sex unions.

What about "blessing" same-sex unions? When I raised this issue in my home church, the committee that reviewed my resolution asked me to define "blessing" in that context. I replied that that is not my term. It is the term used by pastors who do it. I have no idea what is intended by it. I asked, in turn, what they (and those who advocate it) intend by such a blessing. I am still waiting for a response. The ELCA is not clearly defining such "blessing", either, not in anything I have come across.

Are we saying we think it's wonderful, just as we do when a young man and a young woman marry? Are we saying that the fact that it cannot possibly produce progeny in the normal way is also something of which we approve? Are we saying that Lutheran Social Services will make it a policy to place adoptive children in same-sex homes? Will the mothers of those children have any say in that? Will the fathers? The grandparents? What will we do when those "unions" break up? Will we "re-bless" each new pairing? Are we saying that a young woman who confides her lesbian tendencies to her pastor will be encouraged to find a female spouse, rather than to look into reparative therapies? Will "Communities of Grace" be allowed to continue? Will any reparative, re-orienting therapies be a part of the ELCA's social services? What will we teach children about their sexual orientation, either by suggestion (in illustrations, as characters in books and videos, etc.) or by direct sex education?

On the issue of ordaining non-celibate pastors and other rostered persons, the same questions and more apply. Will we declare it a '"right" for any ELCA member who goes through seminary to be a pastor? What grounds do we have for that? Will we expunge the "offensive" passages from scripture? Will we leave them in our Bibles, but just not ever preach on them? What will be the new teaching about the use of scripture? Will we still hold to our confessional belief that the Word is our basic authority for salvation and the Christian life? Or is there a new form of Biblical criticism perhaps already being taught in the seminaries? Considering the high incidence of priestly and pastoral abuse, particularly of boys, what safe-guards will be in place to protect our children? Will ELCA insurance rates increase with the addition of significant numbers of people with significantly higher rates of serious disease and lower life expectancies?

We have a rhino by the horn, here, and we are meeting it without armor. The consequences of our actions are out there in the dark, waiting for us.

We know what the ELCA is saying about a possible federal marriage amendment to define marriage as the union of one man and one woman. It's officially against it. (See "Especially about the Future.") I predicted that would happen before my congregation in May of 2003, and I'm no Jeanne Dixon.

While we're bragging about predictions, the word on the ELCA street is that the Task Force will come out for "local option." Remember, we still don't know what the resolution will actually say. That will be good, won't it? Give us all some time to think about it. Postpone the decision another two years.

What that will actually do is sanction what is going on right now, against ELCA principle, with the approval (at least the silent consent) of bishops and pastors all over the country. We will get *de facto* blessing and ordination, and in two more years the Task Force can say, "No big deal, folks. We've been doing it forever. How about just giving us your official okay." Of course it has the advantage for headquarters of (maybe) keeping the money coming in awhile longer, till they figure out what to do when their actions finally hit home.

These are internal issues. Nobody on your block who plays golf every Sunday is interested in what we in the church define as sin, or what qualifications we require for the ministry. In the society at large, where the federal marriage amendment is the big issue, just as in the church, no one wants to talk about the consequences of homo-sexuality. We just want to talk about how nice it is when any two people commit themselves to each other.

The church has a mission to the disadvantaged, the neglected, the vulnerable in society. That mission is two-fold. We are commissioned to preach the Word to them, that the Holy Spirit may do His work. We are to bring aid, comfort and help. Homosexuals *can* be helped. Thousands have been. Of those who enter reorientation therapy, one third are successful, one third are partially successful and one-third are not helped, the same rate of success as for other psychological conditions.

Twenty years from now, will there be a group lobbying the church crying: Where were you when we needed you? Where were you when I was told that I was born this way, and nothing could be done about it? You told me I should celebrate it, and now I am dying at forty. Where were you when my homosexual father molested me and you told me I must be mistaken because Christian homosexuals never do such things?. Where were you when I sent my daughter to seminary and she came home with a lesbian lover—from seminary? Where were you when we needed support for marriage in Congress, and now marriage hardly exists? Where were you when our right to practice our faith was limited by federal law, and parts of the Bible were declared hate speech, illegal in this country?

In the meantime, we have also a mission to homosexuals themselves. We are sympathetic for the gay or lesbian who comes, like me, to church, to hear the Word and give thanks for it. We have compassion for members who feel caught and betrayed by the ELCA in these matters, but don't know where to turn. We admire the pastors and those bishops (the few, the proud, the brave) who speak against the direction the church is taking. The ELCA leadership makes it very uncomfortable to speak for one man-one woman monogamous sexual unions—marriages, in traditional language. The issue is critical. Consider this a Gray Line Tour. My hope is that you are encouraged to read more in better sources than this.

James Nestingen, professor of church history at Luther Seminary, sums up the position of those of us who oppose these changes: "The church exists for one purpose, to declare Holy Absolution, to speak Christ's forgiving word, the justification of the godless in its preached and sacramental forms. There has always been a special dimension to this promise for those who have been caught up in their own sexuality. So the ELCA has committed itself to a special welcome for gays and lesbians.

But just for that reason, just because of the justification wrought in Christ Jesus, the church has to challenge all other justification schemes." Referencing Wolfart Pannenburg, he goes on: ". . .a church that rejects the traditional teaching on homosexual practice cannot be either evangelical or Lutheran, no matter what it calls itself."[10]

Especially about the Future

We all know how difficult it is to predict events, and still we can't resist. It's part of making plans. From a nervous guess about the weather tomorrow to a hopeful assessment of the chances of landing a particular job, we all engage in predictions. Jesus cautioned us not to be anxious about what we are to eat or to wear. We try to take that to heart. That, it appears to me, is an admonition to refrain from *worry,* a command to live in confidence in God's blessed intentions for us.

It is not a commandment that we make no preparations for needs and events that we can realistically foresee. We know we're going to have to eat again tomorrow. To that end, grocery shopping may be on the docket today. The foolish virgins knew the bridegroom would be coming, but they failed to prepare. They were left in the dark outside. The irresponsible steward hid the money his master had entrusted to him, failing to take advantage of the gain that might come from investing it. His master was furious.

We must think of tomorrow, not with worry, but with resolve, well informed and well prepared.

There is plenty of evidence about what the leaders in the ELCA are doing to prepare our tomorrows. Based on that evidence, we can light our lamps and invest our resources. The big issue this coming year is the sexual question. What is marriage? What should be the sexual standards for our pastors and staffs? How should we lead in the culture on this matter of sexual orientation? How will the ELCA vote on marriage and homosexuality issues in 2005?

The official answer is usually a version of, "We don't really know what is going to happen. We're just waiting for wisdom. We have no agenda."

The official version does not square with ELCA actions. One after another, the following items tell a story. They are presented, with sources, without comment.

Current ELCA Policy and Practice, as quoted in Journey Together Faithfully, Part Two, ELCA Studies on Sexuality:

The ELCA has no policy on the blessing of same-sex unions. In 1993 the Conference of Bishops stated that they did not approve an official ceremony by the church for the blessing of same-sex unions because they found no basis for it in the Bible or in tradition. Statements of the bishops do not establish policy for the church but do shape its understandings and practice.

It is the policy of the ELCA that all single rostered people, including those who understand themselves to be homosexual, are expected to abstain from sexual relationships.

Lutherans Concerned/North America web site, February 22, 2004 press release:

In a move certain to create ripples in the religious community, Bethany Lutheran Church in Minneapolis has voted overwhelmingly to call and ordain as pastor a gay man who is living in a committed relationship. Bethany is a congregation of the ELCA and plans to ordain Jay Wiesner, who has been serving for nearly two years as the congregation's "pastoral minister" for outreach.

. . . The action would be contrary to ELCA protocols, because the ELCA accepts homosexual men or women as pastors only if

they promise to remain celibate. It would be the first such Lutheran ordination in the Upper Midwest since 2001 when a Saint Paul congregation ordained a lesbian woman as pastor.

Text of sermon by Herbert Chilstrom, formerly presiding bishop of the ELCA, delivered at a Lutherans Concerned worship service at St. James Episcopal Church, Milwaukee, Wisconsin, Friday, August 15, 2003:

Have we come to the time when God is calling the church to change its ways by welcoming homosexual persons into full membership—opening every door of privilege and opportunity?. . .I can only speak for myself. Yes, the time has come. In fact, it is long, long overdue.

Lutherans Concerned press release, September 13, 2003:

Lutherans Concerned/North America, Lutherans Concerned/Twin Cities, Minneapolis & Saint Paul Area Synod (ELCA) Joint committee for Ministry to and with Gay and Lesbian persons their Families and Friends, and Wingspan Ministry of St Paul-Reformation Lutheran Church announce the North American Reconciling in Christ Conference and Biennial Assembly of Lutherans Concerned/North America to be held July 22-25, 2004, at Augsburg College, Minneapolis, MN. . . .conference attendees will be able to work on sexuality within the Evangelical Lutheran Church in America (ELCA). Major decisions will hinge on the outcome of this study, especially the blessing of same-gender unions and rostering of otherwise qualified persons in committed gay or lesbian relationships.

Local Option for Certifying Pastors, essay by George H Muedeking, D.D., Ph. D. (Dr. Muedeking is Editor of FOCL-POINT, newsletter of the Fellowship of Confessing Lutherans, www.foclnews.org) retired after 14 years as Editor of the Lutheran Standard, the official publication of the American

Lutheran Church. He was also Professor of Functional Theology at Pacific Lutheran Theological Seminary, Berkeley, California.) About the so-called local option idea:

[*Presiding Bishop Mark] Hanson gave this strategy a very neutral sounding name: "Ordination to place." That is, the ELCA would not have to take a stand on the issue of homosexual practice, one way or the other. But the homosexually active prospective ordinand would seek out a bishop, a congregation, a synod, sympathetic to his or her case. In that place and for that kind of ministry, the ordination would occur and everyone would be satisfied. Those indignant at what was done, would be mollified, since it was not their synod, congregation or bishop that had welcomed this clergy type. And certainly the proponents would rejoice for achieving their purpose of opening the clergy roster of the ELCA to this kind of minister and ministry. These could look forward to continuing to wear down the opposition like water dripping on a stone. . . . The perception is growing rapidly across the ELCA that he and the homosexuality study committee appointed by him to bring in to the 2005 CWA an action-resolution will propose this solution as a way out of the disastrous turmoil that is ahead if the Assembly votes to certify to its roster the homosexually active. . . . The ominous prospect of a church-wide revolt is too real, a mass defection too likely that any action, for or against, by the 2005 Church Wide Assembly, will split the church. Either way, those following the biblical principles of sexual conduct, or those pushing the envelope to revise our millennia-old moral insights, will walk out.*

Fellowship of Confessing Lutherans Website, accessed July 21, 2004:

Bishop Peter Rogness lifted censure on two congregations which violated ELCA policy vis a vis *same-sex ordinations—Reformation Lutheran—the congregation which ordained Anita Hill, and Hosanna! Lutheran—on January 15, 2003 in the St. Paul Synod with the following announcement: 'As we begin a new year I am hopeful we might also be about the business of creating a more open and affirming posture toward those ministries (such as Hosanna! And St. Paul-Reformation) which have pressed the edges of our pattern of life together.' No, in case the reader is wondering, those congregations did not alter their stances or repudiate their actions.*

Soulforce Press Release: July 29, 2003:

The National Lutheran Youth Organization, an official youth office of the Evangelical Lutheran Church in America (ELCA), voted overwhelmingly to welcome people of all sexual orientations as members. Delegates also approved a resolution supporting the blessing of same-sex unions and the ordination of non-celibate individuals of all sexual orientations in committed relationships. The ELCA currently will not ordain non-celibate homosexuals as pastors.

Lutheran Lesbian and Gay Ministries (LLGM)

Mission Partners listed on the LLGM website who receive financial support from LLGM include seven pastors and two churches, all rostered ELCA persons and ELCA congregations. It also lists six ELCA pastors who formerly received such support, and two more ELCA churches. Current and former Extraordinary Candidacy Project ministers and congregations include three churches and five pastors, all ELCA. (Extraordinary Candidacy Project is a group that advocates for gays and lesbians who wish to become rostered ELCA pastors.) It claims that in November of 2002, twelve ELCA congregations and three independent Lutheran congregations were being served by ECP pastors, four ECP approved seminary graduates had been ordained and installed in ELCA congregations in the previous two years, and that members of ECP serve now in churches in eight states.

Excerpts from the Newsletter of the Fellowship of Evangelical Lutheran Laity and Pastors, Summer 1985. (Commenting and reporting on actions by the Committee for a New Lutheran Church, CNLC, and on the LCA convention: **This was prior to the formation of the ELCA.)**

. . .a Biblically-based resolution was put forward which called for the church to provide 'Ministry of Healing for Gay and Lesbian People. . .to withdraw from a homosexual life-style.' This resolution . . . was defeated.

. . .a resolution opposed to pre-marital sex. . .reaffirmed Jesus' and the New Testament's opposition to fornication. This resolution. . .was defeated.

Within the year Bishop Lowell Erdahl has spoken at two pro-gay rallies. In September 1984 he spoke at a commissioning service for "Lutherans Concerned" (a group working for the acceptance of homosexuality in the Lutheran church). The service was held at St. Paul Reformation Lutheran Church (LCA) in St. Paul, Minnesota—the church famous for its 'gay blessing'. ... held hands and exchanged declarations of commitment', after which Pastor Paul Tidemann invoked God's blessing on the relationship.

Excerpts from an Associated Press story as it appeared in the Longmont, Colorado *Times-Call*, June 5, 2004:

. . .a letter to Congress that it was not government's job to enshrine laws reflecting a specific religious view [stating "We believe the federal marriage amendment reflects a fundamental disregard for the individual civil rights and ignores differences among our nation's many religious traditions. It should be rejected," they wrote this week. . . .Karen Vagley of the Lutheran Office of Governmental Affairs of the Evangelical Lutheran Church in America said her group signed the letter because "we see this as a civil rights matter. Our social statements are clear: we do not discriminate."

Excerpts from a letter from Herbert Chilstrom and Peter

Rogness (former bishop and current bishop in the ELCA) taken from the internet on February 28, 2004:

Like [Rogness] I am convinced that voting on the proposed issue in 2005 is inadvisable. All sides will lose if we proceed with the vote.

Can we let those congregations who want to seek new ways of ministering to gay and lesbian people do that without making a new church policy?

Can we let otherwise qualified candidates be approved if there are congregations wanting to call them, and synods and candidacy committees who know them and believe they will enhance the ministry of the church—without presuming to change in one sweeping vote the long-held views of the church?

New York Times, October 23, 2003:

ELCA pastor Barbara Lundblad, non-celibate lesbian, officiated at a marriage of two lesbians in New York City October 17, 2003. Her bishop refused to discipline her. He said same-sex blessings are neither "precluded or encouraged" in ELCA Definitions and Guidelines for Discipline.

From Hope Lutheran (ELCA), Cleveland, Ohio church bulletin, September 2003:

Hope Lutheran hosts the Cleveland Chapter of Lutherans Concerned gay and lesbian community. . .Rev. Barbara Lundblad will be our guest speaker. Rev. Lundblad, from Union Theological Seminary, NY., has been the Lutheran preacher to the Protestant Hour radio program since 1983; has served on the church council of the ELCA; and was on the commission for a new church/ELCA.

Action of the Minneapolis Synod Assembly , June 2004:

Jen Nagel, a non-rostered, non-celibate lesbian serving as "pastor" at Salem English Lutheran Church (ELCA) in Minneapolis was elected to the Synod Council of the Minneapolis Synod. Her partner, Jane McBride, is a UCC pastor. Minneapolis Area Synod is the largest synod (by population) in the ELCA.

Excerpts from a Letter from Christopher Mbuga of ELCT (Tanzania) to James Torgerson, editor of The Lutheran Commentator, January 30, 2004:

I am a student at Wartburg Seminary in Dubuque, Iowa. I am an ordained clergy of the ELCTanzania/North Western Diocese, and at present . . .working on a Masters of Sacred Theology degree. . . .I am . . .aware of some of the . . .controversial issues the church has grappled with . . Homosexuality concerned me the most, and I am not sure what the future holds for us, the ELCTanzania, with regards to our companionship with the ELCA.

Excerpts from a Letter from Pastor Kris Nyman to his parish in Beulah, North Dakota, Zion Lutheran, ELCA (printed with permission):

This is my final report on the ELCA National Assembly. . . .there were many good, even great things that happened at the Assembly. . . .Unfortunately, for all the good things . . .the bad things were so significant that they cast a pall over the good things.

Some of the worship was heretical such as the following:. "God our Mother, you are the matrix of our power, our tenderness, and our courage. We forget too often that you are God. (response):Holy is your name." Nowhere in Scripture is God addressed as mother. This is goddess worship. God has characteristics which are softer, like where Jesus says "I would have gathered you as a hen gathers her chicks under her wings, but you would not". But Jesus constantly referred to God as Father, never as Mother. . . .[it continued] "In our friends and lovers, our spouses and children (Response): We see you coming with power." There is only one reason why lovers are distinguished separately from spouses. This is GLBT people asserting their influence in worship. This is heresy. . . .The resolution to adhere to the time line of voting in 2005 to bless GLBT unions and to ordain openly practicing GLBT pastors was one of the most intense times during the National Assembly. Many voting members debated that it does not makes sense to decide in 2005 on the specifics of the GLBT issue before we have the general social statement on human sexuality due out in 2007. The Assembly voted to adhere to the time line.

As this vote was being taken and at other times, the GLBT people who were not Voting Members, and could not be on the floor where the Voting Members sat, would surround the perimeter of the voting area and stand quietly, while the debating and voting was taking place. They also stood outside the entryway that all voting members had to go in and out of. They always stood in staggered positions so you had to weave your way through them.

. . .There has been no change in the ELCA's direction since CCM was agreed upon in Denver 1999. For the past 4 years many of us in the Synod, and for the past 2 years many of us at Zion have been working for reform in the church.

We have tried many ways to make our voices heard. We have withheld benevolence, put the Search Team to work, had Bishop Danielson speak to us, held forums, prayed, and worked to pass resolutions for reform at both the Synod and the National Assemblies. Still there has not been the slightest hint of reform or change of direction in the ELCA.

The Lutheran Commentator, July-September 2003, p 4:

"*How gay outcome was achieved at LYO [Lutheran Youth Organization]*

Kevin Maly, a gay ELCA pastor from Denver who is on the ELCA Task Force on Homosexuality, was a workshop leader at the Lutheran Youth Organization convention in Atlanta, July 2003. Erin Clark, also pro-gay and on the Task Force on Homosexuality, led the workshop. Bob Gibeling, Program Director for the GLBT Caucus, Lutherans Concerned/North America, attended the workshop and participated in the discussion. No opposing views were part of the presentation!

After the pro-gay session with ELCA leaders, the LYO passed a resolution that it supports the blessings of same-sex unions and the ordination of non-celibate individuals in committed relationships of all sexual orientations.

Is this one-sided program an accident? No. Jim Childs, Director of the Task Force on Homosexuality, assisted in planning this program (Pre-Assembly Report, V, p.4)

Press release July 29, 2003 from Soulforce, a "network of friends . . .seeking justice for God's Lesbian, Gay, Bisexual and Transgender Children":

The Lutheran Alliance for Full Participation and Soulforce, Inc. comment on the ELCA youth office for taking this stand, and encourage youth of the ELCA to join with them in vigiling, leafleting, and nonviolence trainings throughout the year before the ELCA Churchwide Assembly, August 11-17.

By a 91% margin, the youth organization also voted to be listed as a 'Reconciled in Christ' organization with Lutherans Concerned/North America, an independent group of gay, lesbian, bisexual and transgender Lutherans, and one of the GLBT coalition groups of the Lutheran Alliance for Full Participation.

First Things, June/July 2004, Number 144, p. 77:

A study on sexuality is scheduled to come to a vote at the 2005 churchwide assembly of the Evangelical Lutheran Church in America (ELCA). My Lutheran friends tell me that the revisionists have been watching carefully the Episcopalian crack-up and want to avoid the alienation of a couple of million members from the much larger ELCA. So the idea is being floated that a vote would be unnecessarily "divisive", that love requires that we live with our differences. Over time after a few thousand same-sex blessings (which may by then be legally recognized as marriages) and a few hundred ordinations of practicing gays and lesbians (at first tolerated as 'exceptions'), the Lutheran traditions will be de facto transformed from legalism to grace, and all without the inconvenient difficulties of formal deliberation, debate, and decision.

The strategy might very well work. Never underestimate the power of anti-nomianism veiled in the language of love. When truth is trimmed to accommodate togetherness, the quality of togetherness is admittedly thinned, but the good thing is that nobody is excluded. Except, of course, those who thought the idea was to be together in truth. The churchwide assembly is still a year away. It is enough time to effectively label those who want a vote for fidelity as the party of "divisiveness".

Commentary on article above by Pastor Dan Hansen, Longmont, CO: (printed with permission.)

The author is predicting that the ELCA may very well try to pull the 2005 vote off the table because they believe it will be 'too divisive', but that they will continue to look the other way as gay pastors and gay couples are ordained-despite current ELCA prohibitions. Over time, it will just become the accepted thing.

The ELCA's movement in this direction is a modern day example of 'anti-nomianism', which is a theology of 'anything goes. . .we are now free from the law of Moses!' But, as Jesus proclaimed in Mt 5:17, 'Do not think that I have come to abolish the Law or the Prophets: I have not come to abolish them but to fulfill them.' In other words, the laws of Moses (especially the Ten Commandments) still provide guidance for our lives. (They have not become the 'TEN SUGGESTIONS.')

The author is also predicting that those of us who might push for a vote in 2005 (so that the ELCA might take a stand on these issues) will therefore probably be then labeled as "divisive"?

"One of the key questions for us as the ELCA will be: "What is of higher value to us—truth or unity?"

Letter from a participant in the <u>Journeying Together Faith-</u>

fully to his pastor, October 24, 2003 (name withheld):

I finally lost my patience with 'Some people think. . .on the other hand, others think. . .' We have listened to that every evening. All opinions are of equal value. We must kindly consider the opinions of every practicing, homosexual activist and we must not be judgmental under any circumstance. I'm sure that the Devil himself would be listened to carefully by 'reasonable' Lutherans. . . .Published research data no longer has any value. If the homosexual juggernaut does not like the results of scientific research they simply say it's not really correct. And when a huge research effort to find the homosexual gene fails and is discontinued, they put out the word that 'maybe' we have now found it! Why not 'Some people believe that Jesus Christ rose from the dead, . . .others think that the apostles had hallucinations.' All opinions must be carefully considered.

I probably take a different view than most . . .in that I worry so much about the broader consequences of current developments. What is going to happen to my country if this trend continues? The churches should be the leaders in resisting these developments, not leading them. Some of them are, thank God, but not the mainline churches. And those churches that are taking a strong stand are growing and vital today but are regularly demonized by the press.

NY Times, October 19, 2003, fashion/wedding section:

Anna Marie Vigen and Alison Anne Strickler affirmed their partnership Friday in the James Chapel at Union Theological Seminary in New York. The Rev. Barbara Kay Lundblad, a Lutheran minister who is an associate professor there, performed the commitment ceremony

Ms. Vigen is 35. She is a doctoral candidate in Christian social and theological ethics at the seminary. She graduated magna cum laude from St. Olaf College in Northfield, Minn., and received a master's degree in ethics awarded jointly by the Pacific Lutheran Theological Seminary and the Graduate Theological

Union, both in Berkeley, Calif..

Ms. Vigen's father, the Rev. David C. Vigen, lives in Iowa City, where he retired as the pastor of Christ the King Lutheran Church. Her mother, Dr. Kathryn L. Vigen of Chicago, is the director of nursing and a professor at North Park University School of Nursing there.

Ms. Strickler, 33, is the director of marketing for Mathews Nielsen landscape architects in New York. She also makes handmade books and albums. She graduated from Rutgers. She is a daughter of the Rev. Warren Strickler and Mrs. Strickler of Harrisonburg, Va. Her father, who retired in l993 as the pastor of the First Lutheran Church in Kearny, N. J., is now a minister at St. Paul Lutheran Church in Mount Solon, Va. Her mother, Joan Strickler, retired as the admissions officer for the Graduate School of Management at the Rutgers University School of Business, Newark.

How Homosexuals Are Changing the Church, by Linda Harvey, published on Kairo_News@yahoo groups.com, May 19, 2003.

. [I attended]. Trinity Lutheran Seminary [ELCA] in Columbus, Ohio. . . I was a new student. . . The professor of Old Testament studies. . .was single and lived with another woman. . .I soon became convinced that she was, in violation of the ELCA regulations for ordained ministers, a practicing lesbian.

"Homosexuality is a sin," she read. Out of forty students in class, I and three others moved to the right wall, indicating that we agreed. . . .From that day on, I never felt like I was in step with the seminary. . . .what I saw and heard in this 'Christian' institution was hard at times to believe.

It was about this time that the national ELCA report on human sexuality surfaced, making national headlines with its recommendation that the Lutheran Church reconsider its position on homosexuality and premarital sex. It was all the talk at the school—

mostly in support of the recommendations.

. . .one Trinity faculty member . . .had written in opposition to the ELCA sexuality report. . .I made an appointment with him. . . .He explained how undaunted interpreters of Scripture are by protests that appeal to biblical tradition and apparent meaning.

. . .whatever happened to the authority of God? It's not recognizable at Trinity Lutheran Seminary in any consistent form.

I don't know of any better way to make clear what the ELCA is doing, just out of the line of vision of the average person in the pews, than to list all the items above. They are but a few of the many actual incidents and reports, but they paint a picture. Check the web sites and other sources listed in "Resources" for additional examples. The ELCA is engaged in a charade. It is pretending to be open to various points of view about the sexuality issues (as if the church were not the repository of a well defined and culturally superior point of view from ancient times), while at the same time it engages, on many fronts, as enablers, co-conspirators, and advocates for the GLBT lobby.

Diversity: the Goal that Morphs

True story. In a Chicago suburb a few years ago Leslie Anne's third grade teacher gave her class a number of writing assignments related to a project on family heritage—a way of discovering and sharing ethnic backgrounds in a community of mixed, mostly European descendants. There were a number of children with Slavic and Mediterranean backgrounds, a few Orientals and a few American-born blacks. And Leslie Anne. Her father's people were English as far back as any one knew, and her mother's were Irish. On both sides, the family had been in the U. S. for many generations. After the first few days of the project, after hearing about the exotic foods and customs of some of her classmates' families, Leslie Anne came home despondent.

"We are so boring, Mother! I don't know what to write."

Leslie Anne's mother was a kind and sensitive human being, and she realized that her daughter was feeling left out—vanilla in a room full of zesty spices. So she suggested that the two of them do some phoning and talk to their older relatives—a little genealogical research. In the next few days, Leslie Anne collected a number of wonderful tales of her grandfather in the war, of big events on the farm the family had worked for a hundred years, of the occupations of her various forebears, funny stories about family characters. It was fun, and she found that she had something to share that was interesting and exciting to her classmates.

Our own culture is just that—our own. Normal. Ordinary. Usual. It is what we are and what we do. There is nothing exotic or enticing about it. Except to others. Except to those outside who see us fresh, who see our habits as new ideas, sometimes appealing, sometimes appalling. It is very easy to walk into a diner or church in Fort Morgan, Colorado or O'Neill, Nebraska and accuse the inhabitants of having no culture of value or interest. They are likely to agree with you. We don't think of the way we keep house or the games our children play or the songs we hum as we work or the proverbs we shout when something goes wrong as *culture.* When we make sure the kids' faces are clean and their hair is combed before they go to school—is that culture? When we bow our heads habitually before meals, is that culture? Is the story of Cinderella culture, or Mother Goose rhymes, or roasting chillies on the grill every autumn? Are two-week family camping trips, choir tours, rodeos, county fairs, garage sales, taking food to a family whose father has just died—are those cultural activities? If culture means anything, they are. And if culture means anything, it is normal that we do those things, share those things, without thinking much about their place in our culture.

In a world clamoring for *cultural diversity,* step one should be defending the cultural patterns, habits, literature, music and folklore that we already own—each of us. It may mean cutting out some elements that are mean and unnecessary. We can quit calling Brazil nuts "nigger toes" and Italians "wops" (it originally stood for "without papers"—interesting sidelight). Our culture can benefit by a little editing, as can *any* culture. It can also benefit from a little intentional appreciation of what we have and what we are. I do not need to apologize for being a faded blonde Anglo Saxon of a certain age, any more than the eight-year-old across the street from me needs to apologize for being a tall, athletic, Chinese-born little girl adopted by a pair of American parents.

We have a culture that has for centuries valued and respected women. Our little girls have always gone to school along with our little boys. Our daddies open doors for women, rush to lift heavy things to save women's weaker bodies, slide chairs in for their sweethearts at the restaurants. Women can own property among us, and have been known to homestead alone, to become physicians in pioneer country, to own and manage businesses, and their men tend to admire them for it. This is a very quaint attitude in some cultures.

In the Tokyo railway station, among all those people, a handsome and well-dressed man of some sixty years walks confidently down the concourse headed for the train. About ten feet behind him, a smaller woman of about the same age wears soft- sided bags on each shoulder and pulls a gigantic suitcase, watching her husband carefully, and moving as fast as she can. Men in that culture do not carry parcels. Their women do. That is changing somewhat today, but it is the traditional way. Interesting and amusing to observe, it is not a pattern in which I would wish to participate. I think it is a quaint attitude.

Our culture is like many others in that our celebrations center on food and family. We have Thanksgiving feasts, Christmas smorgasbords, picnics on the Fourth of July and at family reunions. Our foods, labeled boring by food editors, are much sought after by people from other cultures. I entertained some foreign guests at my table a few years ago. Their son, whom they were visiting, was a graduate student here in Colorado who had been living with me as he learned English. When I asked him what he would like me to serve for dinner, he immediately replied "Thanksgiving turkey! And pie. But please bake some chocolate chip cookies, too." I agreed, of course. When, late in the evening, we sat drinking coffee and eating chocolate chip cookies, his mother asked (through her son) if she could have the cookies. He translated for me, and I thought he meant that she wanted the recipe. I said I could write it immediately. But no, she didn't want the recipe. She wanted the cookies! So I boxed up the whole batch and sent them back to the hotel with them. Later I learned that there is no oven in their home. She doesn't bake. Japanese kitchens rarely have ovens. It's not a matter of wealth or poverty. It's a cultural difference.

We live in a culture currently that has made *diversity* a fetish, if not a religion.

Diversity is simply a synonym for *variety*, as in "the spice of life". As children in the Forties we were taught to wonder at the great diversity of creation—an awe that has never left me. Sameness becomes stale, so for instance, we like a variety in our menus We like several shirts to rotate. We've gone to Minnesota for three vacations in a row and we'd prefer to do something different this year. Among the many varieties of nature, there are the varieties of human beings. The variation among people, note, is considerably more limited than among mammals generally, or than among trees or climates or, even more absurd, insects. People come in a range of colors from the darkest brown to the palest yellowish pinkish tan, but any artist can tell you that this is a very narrow color range. Our internal workings, our muscles, our brains, our diseases and physical requirements are nearly identical across the broad spectrum of humanity. We are in all cases more alike than different; we have more in common than not.

We are very naturally interested in one another, for whatever we learn is a part of our own human history. It is the study of man in all his diversity that has spawned literature, art, all the so-called social sciences, history, geography, economics, philosophy, politics, government, architecture, travel, and so on.

Diversity, then, is not so much a goal to be achieved as it is a *basic condition* of the world and all its inhabitants and locales.

Celebrating cultural differences, while it sounds like a party, is actually a brain-washing technique. Perhaps I should say it is a brain-numbing technique. It is perfectly clear to anybody watching any *diversity fair* that nobody is celebrating patriotic, family-centered, Puritan work-ethic, religious American culture.

The purveyors of diversity as a *good* to be encouraged and promoted are impatient with the foregoing description. They are uninterested in diversity as a description of "the way things are." For them, no group or activity is *perfect* unless it contains "representatives" of all the "relevant diverse groups", and perfection of that sort is their aim. From this notion, we have spawned affirmative action, which seems likely to live way past any defensible equalizing goal. The diversity movement engages instead in various schemes to include "minorities" among college classes, clubs and organizations, and in a number of controls designed to customize and regulate free association among people—a literal contradiction in terms.

I may think that the current preoccupation with this limited kind of diversity is silly (and I do) but I am not so confused or so naïve as to imagine that it will go away soon. It is one of the givens of the current culture, immune from scientific inquiry, logic, any understanding of human nature or the American dream of a nation in which all are equal under the law, and law is no respecter of persons or groups. It has the momentum of revealed truth in a culture that does not believe it believes in revealed truth.

What has this to do with us as Christians, as Lutherans, as believers in a just and loving and merciful God? That is what I would like to know.

"the goal that, within the first ten years of its existence, ten percent of this church's membership would be African American, Asian, Hispanic, or Native American."

—From A Social Statement: *Freed in Christ: Race, Ethnicity and Culture,* adopted by the ELCA August 31, 1993, Kansas City Missouri Churchwide Assembly.

Then God said, 'Let us make man in our image, in our likeness . . .' Gen. 1:26 – NIV

I say to you that many will come from the east and the west, and will take their places at the feast with Abraham. Matt. 8:11 – NIV

He said to them *'Go into all the world and preach the good news to all creation.* Mark 16:15 – NIV

Do not be afraid. I bring you good news of great joy that will be for all the people. Luke 2:10 – NIV

For my eyes have seen your salvation, which you have prepared in the sight of all people. Luke 2:30 – NIV

The Christ will suffer and rise from the dead on the third day, and repentance and forgiveness of sins will be preached in his name to all nations. Luke 24:46-47 – NIV

Father, the time has come. Glorify your Son, that your Son may glorify you. For you granted him authority over all people that he might give eternal life to all those you have given him. John 17:1-2 – NIV

Acts 8:26-40: *Philip is sent to save the Ethiopian eunuch.*

Acts 10:1-43: *The Italian centurion Cornelius is sent to Peter.*

Do nothing out of selfish ambition or vain conceit, but in hu-

mility consider others better than yourselves. Phil. 2:3 – NIV

Does scripture establish quotas for grace or salvation?

Reading the whole ELCA statement on ethnicity, race and culture, it seems clear that negative prejudice is the evil that the church is addressing there. As it should. In the society, the diversity movement has grown up partly out of the same concern. In addition, there appears to be a societal belief that all cultural patterns and forms are not only interesting, but worthy of preservation – that in fact, their preservation is necessary. Why it is necessary is not crystal clear.

In a church that is growing, reaching out to its neighborhood and community, preaching the Gospel, and serving the needy, when the church headquarters intervene to say that that's all very well, but your diversity percentages are not what they should be, is that helpful? Where all those sinful saints and saintly sinners are daily learning to see their fellow members, not as "representatives" of some minority, but as individual people whom God loves and longs to save, as those we are commanded to love as we love ourselves, must we now see them as something other than that? Is there anything, really, that is *more?*

To be fair, the church is not asking that each congregation satisfy those percentage goals. Its aim is that the denomination achieve those goals. It is still a strange goal for a Christian church. Our goal is to bring the good news of the Gospel to all. In practical terms, each congregation reaches out to those in its geographical area. It might sponsor a mission church farther afield, and that might have a targeted neighborhood that is quite different culturally. Each of us as individuals is called to witness to those among whom we live, whom we meet. We are called, it seems to me, to witness to anyone we meet without regard for his color or sex, his political affiliation, his economic or social status, how he dresses, what he does for a living or what he eats. That's enough of a challenge—more (and better) than any quota asks.

And now, God bless Richard John Neuhaus, just as I need him. He quotes Presiding Bishop Mark Hanson:

It better trouble us that the ELCA is still 94 percent descendants of European immigrants in this wonderfully rich and pluralistic country.

Then Neuhaus comments:

Bearing the cross of Scandinavian or German ancestry is not easy. The ELCA leadership suffers from a deep sense of guilt about being noninclusive in a wondrously inclusive culture. Guilt about being noninclusive is joined to the galling realization that there are not a lot of people interested in being included in the ELCA. . . .Since it is improbable that millions of blacks, Latinos, or Filipinos are going to join up any time soon, it seems that, for the members of the ELCA, salvation must be by faith alone, combined with profound contrition for being who they are. . . They and their church would, I expect, be more generally appreciated were they not so touchingly eager to catch up with the cutting edge of a culture to which the community of faith is to be not a mirror but a contrast.[11]

Neuhaus is right. The ELCA does seem to be embarrassed about its heritage. How strange. While we encourage others to "discover" and "celebrate" and "preserve" their heritage, as a church we seek to subdue and hide our own. The ELCA embarrassment is mostly confined to headquarters. Out here among the congregations, we still enjoy our German and Scandinavian foods; we take trips to visit the "old country;" we sing hymns that our fathers sang. That is not all we do, nor does it color our daily lives all that much. Certainly not enough to drive away potential Lutherans. For the decline in our numbers, we must look elsewhere.

Is there any evidence that an appreciation for, and devotion to, diversity erases prejudice? Is *culture*, any culture, eternal? Should it be? Can we, should we, consciously regulate culture, or try to prevent cultural patterns from disappearing? Are all cultures and cultural patterns equal and equally worthy of preservation? Is there such a thing as a Christian culture? If so, how does it look?

It is perfectly obvious that a concern with diversity teaches people how to count. The question is, does it teach them how to love?

Where Did All the Daddies Go?

Are there any ELCA toes still untrodden in these pages? Let's see if we can fix that.

Last night we took a dear ninety-three-year-old of our acquaintance out to dinner. A young couple with two little ones came and sat near us. Mommy and the two little girls looked pretty normal, but Daddy's head was shaved in a very long and curly Mohawk. His body was well pierced and his shorts hung fashionably and nervously low. He spent some of his time leaning his head on his wife's shoulder, looking for all the world like a lap dog. At one point Esther leaned toward us across the table and said (too loudly to make me comfortable) "When Harry and I were young, men were more *male*, do you know what I mean?" We did.

Some years ago, our church started asking women to participate in ushering at worship. When the church called to ask me if I'd be on the list I said, "No." There was a startled silence on the line, then a cautious, "Why ever not?" I explained that practically all of our Sunday School teachers, the entire altar guild, several Bible study circles, the kitchen committee, the food response committee and even our janitor at the time were women. "Let the men keep on ushering. It's a manly thing to do, and they ought to do it." No stars after my name on the time and talent sheet.

I really don't object to women ushering. Women pastors do not constitute a violation either of our theology, our history or decorum. I think it's well that women serve on church councils and men are helping with the food committee these days. But men should still be men in the church as elsewhere, and women should be women. We need the masculine virtues particularly in the church. In an age when so many of our children have no fathers in the house, there should be fathers in God's house. Our children, especially our boys, need to see that it's a good thing to be male. They need to see that good strong men pray and sing lustily and participate in Bible study. If they are lucky, they may also see daddies who lead family devotions as well as mow the lawn and enforce curfews. Men must not be subdued or sent to the back of the church bus.

The church should never be "a woman's place" or "a man's place" exclusively. It is good if it is a family place, if for no other reason than that the body of Christ is so often described in family terms, as is our Lord: God the father, Christ our brother, the church the bride of Christ, and so on.

The church is in danger of over-feminization. Hymns and prayers addressed to "Our Mother God" are not helpful. Eliminating masculine language in the Bible is not only irritating, it is emasculating and dishonest besides. I still can't sing the old Christmas carol as "Good Christian Friends Rejoice". Not only is *friends* one of the least singable words in English, it isn't what the original lyricist wrote. Since when do we have the right to rewrite the poetry of others? That is only one example. Others leap out at us every Sunday. I own several original paintings. Do you know that it is illegal for me to alter them in any way—even though I own them? If you write a short story today, can your great-grandchild rewrite it in ninety years to remove the "sexist" language? Would it be morally right if he did? What happens to "Our Father Who art in Heaven"? What do we do with Jesus Christ, God's only begotten *Son*?

God presents Himself to us masculine. The Bible speaks of Him as masculine. We pray to Him as Our Heavenly Father, as Jesus taught us. Does changing all that to suit some new age gender-neutral idea of the universe help us to focus on Christ?

The first question we ask when a baby is born is, "Is it a boy or a girl?" When we meet someone coming toward us on the sidewalk, our unconscious but primary question is "Man or woman"? If we can't tell, and it happens sometimes nowadays, neither can we get the question out of our minds. When gender is obvious, we can relax. We know how to relate to a man, to a woman, to a boy or to a girl. Everything proceeds from that. It is the floor of our cognizance of one another. We find it extremely difficult, if not impossible, to relate to anyone who announces that after the weekend *he* is going to be *Donna*. He/she is still not going to be one of the girls. In these situations sexuality becomes prominent, when of course it should fade immediately into the background so we can get to know each other. To be friends, and not potential sexual partners, we must sublimate sex, and that's very difficult to do when it is so startlingly out of the norm. Humanity is "divided" into two complementary sets. Anything "in the middle" is problematic. So we think of God as He, even though we know full well that He loves us with all the tenderness of the kindest mother. He also loves us with all the sinew of the sternest and most courageous father.

I am sorry. I cannot think of God in gender neutral terms. And Jesus in a denim dress and eye liner is not a possibility either. Jesus in Levis and a plaid shirt is possible. That's the way it is. Changing the language does not change my gut-level perceptions, but it does interfere with my concentration.

In the middle of scripture, or prayer, or a hymn, a neon *she* appears. Now instead of hearing, singing the message, there is a mental short circuit.

The language feminists claim that *he* language is dismissive and degrading of women. It is quite the opposite. Whenever *she* appears in English, it is specific, particular and exclusive *to women. He, man,* and *mankind* are generic and *inclusive.* The poor guys have to share them with everybody. We are *mankind.* We are *all men. She* is exclusive and eliminates *he.*

The last thing we should do in church is eliminate the inclusive *he.*

Hymns in Our Hearts

The agenda for the ELCA Church Wide Assembly in 2005 was not quite full enough. Those folks in Chicago are absolute *beavers*. They work all the time, and always think of more things to do. But then, they are bureaucrats. David Mills describes church bureaucrats beautifully: *They are the sort of friend who "for your own good," weeds your library, changes the settings on your computer, replaces your furniture, and rearranges your finances—and then charges you a large fee for doing so because "we're all in this together".*[12] The ELCA bureaucracy is rewriting the Lutheran Book of Worship. Presumably someone asked for that. Who, I wonder. I would have thought they had enough on their plates without it. But voting on a new book of worship is on the agenda for the 2005 Church Wide Assembly.

The green hymnal and worship book is by now thoroughly familiar to us, both its strengths and its weaknesses. But at Chicago headquarters, familiarity breeds contempt. We have to have a new hymnal and worship book.

If we're going to have a new worship book, if we are going to evaluate such a book in preparation for accepting or rejecting it, we need to think about the uses of a worship book. I know. The new book is almost done. This discussion is a day late and a dollar short. But better late (and short) than never.

Few publications of the church matter more than the worship and hymn book. After scripture itself, the liturgies of our worship and the hymns we sing are the most important teaching tool we have. In the end, they may teach our beliefs more effectively even than the preaching. They get under our skin. We find ourselves humming a tune and then remembering the words and we sing them as we drive or sweep or shower. Hymns are the condensations of attitudes and convictions of the faith. One Sunday recently our pastor asked us all to sing "Jesus Loves Me" in the middle of the sermon. It was appropriate to his message. A number of handkerchiefs came out immediately after. Messing with the hymnody is serious business. It is true also of the liturgy. Those of us who grew up singing or saying the words of the 51st Psalm ("Create in me a clean heart, O God", etc., v. 10 and following, KJV) still long for it, though it hasn't been used in many of our churches for years now.

I remember when the green book came out. A friend of mine was so happy to see that Beethoven's *Ode to Joy*, with the lyrics *Joyful, Joyful, We Adore Thee* was included. It was a favorite of his and its inclusion made up for a lot. We all naturally look for our favorites. We should be thinking, even about our favorites, in terms of our beliefs. Gracia Grindal, Hymnist and Professor of Rhetoric at Luther Seminary, says, "The language of the liturgy is more important to consider than the music, because, when sung, these words become the theology of the people regardless of whether these words are rank heresy. If people like the music, they tend not to pay attention to the words. Thus, we check the words carefully before we set them to music."[13]

It is so true. Hymn R241 in the paperback *Renewing Worship* (a collection of hymns for the proposed new hymnal) has a delightful tune. I found myself humming the tune for days after I first heard it, in spite of the fact that the words are anything *but* Lutheran, and I knew it. The chorus reads: "God will delight when we are creators of justice and joy". Oh my. If we do good, He'll love us. Or perhaps the message is that we *can* actually please God. No need for the cross, at least for the moment. Does that sound like Lutheran theology to you?

The various services are also important. Does the marriage service plainly state that a man and a woman are being married? Can we have a Christian marriage ceremony without that? Do the words of the baptismal service and the service for the Lord's supper affirm that these are gifts from God that actually work in us? Not that they are "sacrifices" to God, or "offerings" to Him?

This is not just a complaint from a few of us who are suffering from ELCA overload. It is a caution that, while hymns and liturgies are not, in themselves, sacred or unchangeable, what they say matters. The proposed new book of worship will tell us a great deal about the direction of the ELCA.

As Others See Us

In my twenty-first year I moved away from eastern Nebraska, where you couldn't stumble without bumping into another Lutheran, to St. Louis, Missouri, just a day's drive from home. But it was a world away, I learned. St. Louis, though it is the home of the Lutheran Church Missouri Synod, is more southern than mid-western in culture. Scandinavians are thin on the landscape, and so, for that matter, are Germans. We found a Lutheran church among the south-side "scrubby Dutch" of St. Louis, pastored by a native of Illinois, a Swede, a mission church of the LCA. But we knew we had left Lutheran country. We lived in a neighborhood populated heavily with reformed Jews. I taught in a school full of Baptists and adherents of the Church of Christ. There was not another Lutheran on the faculty of a rather large suburban high school. My best friend among the faculty was the librarian, also a first-year teacher. One day I was pawing through the books she was discarding from the ancient and neglected collection in the school library. There among them was a little hardbound copy of *Luther's Small Catechism.* I snatched it eagerly.

"Why are you throwing this out? It's in perfect shape."

"Take it if you want it. It's no use in a school library," she replied.

She meant that it was no use anywhere. I loved her dearly, and I respected her Christian faith, but I gradually understood that she looked with suspicion on mine. She grew up in Kentucky, and had never known another Lutheran personally. Lutherans, in the view she had learned from childhood, were very little improvement on Catholics. They baptized babies and sang mournful hymns, drank real wine at Holy Communion, believed that the Lord's Supper was some kind of magic, and were generally a fairly stoic and joyless leaf (not important enough to be a branch) on the True Vine.

Sue had her finger on a lot of what Lutherans look like to Americans in general. They concentrate in the mid-west and upper mid-western states, where their Scandinavian and German grandfathers came in the great migrations of the mid- to late-1800s. There are pockets of Lutherans on the West Coast, again mostly among Scandinavians there, in Texas, where large numbers of Germans settled, and in Pennsylvania and Ohio, where many Lutherans settled in the 1700's. But if you want to go to real Lutheran country, try Minnesota, South Dakota or Iowa. The fact that there *is* such a thing as "Lutheran country" is one of our dubious attributes. Since we are so unevenly distributed around the country, we are mysterious if not invisible in many places. We are, or were till recently, strongly ethnic. That is rapidly being diluted by the marriages of our children, as they participate in the great American melting pot. But still, we have a more European flavor than almost any other American denomination.

The following statistics appear on the ELCA website: we were 5,038,006 baptized members at the end of 2002, in 10,721 congregations, a decrease of 1.21% of baptized members since 2001. Confirmed membership decreased by 37,246 (to 3,757,723) between 2001 and 2002. We are a denomination of roughly five million souls, three million of whom are confirmed members. Between 30-31% of us attend worship on any given weekend. The ELCA has not experienced a gain in membership since 1991, three years after the merger that created it. That is a total decline since 1991 of about 4%, similar to declines in other main-line denominations. At the same time, the U. S. population has been growing.

Lutherans are devoted to baroque music, and particularly to the music of Bach, unlike most any other church. Large numbers of our churches have real pipe organs and several choirs. Vocal music is much beloved among Lutherans, and they are often lusty hymn singers. You can start a hymn *a cappella* in a crowd of Lutherans, and they may break into four-part harmony. Makes chills run up and down the spine. One of the good news-bad news jokes about Lutherans goes like this: the good news is we'll give a standing ovation to any musical performance. The bad news also is that we'll give a standing ovation to any musical performance.

We have a disproportionate number of church history scholars.

We are children of more recent immigrations than most other Europeans in America, mostly from northern Europe.

Chief Justice William Rehnquist of the U. S. Supreme Court holds the highest public office any Lutheran has ever held in the U. S. Outside a few governors in the "Lutheran" states, Lutheran politicians at any level are fairly rare. Yet we vote in greater numbers than many of our neighbors, usually for conservatives.

We give at about the same level as many other main-line Christians. We are great supporters of youth ministries.

Our education level is about average, as is our income level.

We tend to fill up the back pews at church.

Our churches have big kitchens.

We are, today, on average older than the population at large—averaging 59 years of age.

We are in many ways very, very average.

However, we tend to see the world a little differently than our Protestant neighbors. Our deep-rooted understanding of human fallibility and our belief in our complete dependence on God produce certain tics. Do you have them? The women's magazines often print little self-evaluation questionnaires to help readers discover if they are effective parents, or good lovers, or inclined to depression—you know the kind of thing. What would such a test look like if we wanted to know how Lutheran we are?

I believe I can live for 24 hours without sinning.

Self-esteem is a Christian virtue.

The public schools do the best job of instilling family values.

Pastors and bishops are more Christian than laymen.

We are going to eradicate hunger in ten years.

The best church is one that teaches the power of positive thinking.

The best sermons are relevant to the evening news.

When I sin, I must resolve to do better to stay in God's grace.

If you said, "I don't think so" to every one, you may well be incurably Lutheran. Orthodox Lutherans carry their theological cautions into their public endeavors. Some would say we take a dim view of human ability to solve problems. Lutherans are inclined to say we are realistic.

Lutherans recognize a rich tradition and a long history in the faith. While academics are busy removing the works of "dead white males" from the curricula at all levels of education, Lutherans have continued to study the scriptures and the works of early church leaders and thinkers. This tradition is now being rediscovered among some of the more conservative denominations. Currently Intervarsity Press is producing a series of commentaries on the books of the Bible—anthologies actually—of the writings of the early church fathers. Intervarsity is a very respectable evangelical-conservative Christian publishing house. Not so long ago, such a series from such a publisher would have been unlikely. While many Protestants want nothing to do with historical Christianity from the end of the first century until the Reformation, Lutherans, particularly academic Lutherans, have maintained a lively interest in the thought of the medieval church.

Lutherans have a sense of humor about themselves—too much so, some say. We think we are humorous in many ways, but we don't want to be a laughing-stock. Garrison Keillor is not one of our church historians.

When Lutherans leave for another denomination, they go most often to other, more *evangelical* Protestant churches.

All of this is generalization. We are heirs of a great faith and a great tradition, and we are a mystery to many of our fellow Christians. That is nothing to worry about particularly. The real question is not *How Do Others See Us?*, but *Who Are We, Really?* How do we see ourselves?

What Do Lutherans Believe?

Many years ago I was given some advice about teaching which works pretty well for writing too. "Never underestimate your students' intelligence; never over-estimate their background." On the strength of that, of my own study, and with a little help from my friends I dare to summarize Lutheran belief for Lutherans.

If you are a member of a Lutheran church in 2004, chances are a little better than 50/50 that you were born into a Lutheran family and raised in the Lutheran church. A lot of us, then, were not. If you have attended a new-member class in preparation for joining a Lutheran church sometime in the last twenty years, chances are you learned more about the church's programs and activities than about Lutheran doctrine. Just a guess. If you know your Lutheran theology pretty well, it is likely that you occasionally hear a comment at church that sets alarm bells off in your head, and it could be coming from the pulpit.

The Lutheran church has a cohesive theology. We are a *confessional* church. That means that what we believe is agreed upon and written. This is no new age operation where "everybody's truth is honored". The Lutheran church is founded on, first, scripture, after that the historic confessions—the Apostles and the Nicene Creeds, the Augsburg Confession, the Book of Concord and Luther's Large and Small Catechisms. In academic and theological circles, Lutheran scholars are highly regarded. We are heirs to the voluminous and often delightful writings of Martin Luther—his sermons, table talk, commentaries on scripture, and so on.

We are the Church of the Reformation. The great reformer Martin Luther is a magnificent figure whose life is amazing and inspiring to us. He translated the whole of the scripture into the German language, and in the process was instrumental in shaping the modern German language. He, together with the Brothers Grimm, is credited with bringing the many German dialects together into a unified whole. His courage was tremendous. For much of his life he was an outlaw, under edict of the pope. For all of his pastoral life he preached every day and twice on Sunday. He taught at the University of Wittenburg, married and fathered six children, acted as overseer and counselor to parishes throughout the province, in addition to the pastoral duties of attending to the spiritual and physical needs of his parishioners. His sermons are warm and thoughtful, very readable and relevant today. I don't know if every Lutheran *ought* to know about Luther's life, but it seems to me that not knowing is missing something.

Occasionally nowadays someone will say, "We don't worship Martin Luther, you know." Of course not. Lutherans never did, and they are perhaps less likely to now than ever, for they seem to know so little about him. In any case, it is not a matter of worshiping Luther; it is a matter of valuing what he has given us. As a pastor, he was above all concerned to teach the scriptures and the doctrines of the faith.

Early in his pastoral ministry, Luther toured the countryside to discover what the people were being taught. He was appalled at the general ignorance, even among the pastors. He went home and wrote his Small Catechism. It was meant to be a family handbook of the faith, so that any mother and father using it could teach the children and everyone in the household the basic tenets of the faith. Luther's Small Catechism remains one of the classic documents of Christianity today, particularly of course among Lutherans. The Small Catechism contains the Ten Commandments, the Lord's prayer, the Apostles' creed, and what we believe about Holy Baptism and the Lord's Supper. The pattern of the book is simple. One commandment, for example, is stated, followed by an explanation. "You shall not steal. What does this mean for us? We are to fear and love God so that we do not take our neighbor's money or property, or get them in any dishonest way, but help him to improve and protect his property and means of making a living." (From a memorial edition of the catechism issued by the Aid Association for Lutherans in 1979 in observance of the 450th anniversary of its printing.) Luther's Small Catechism is an excellent place to start learning about the faith, whether you are new to Lutheranism, or a long-time member.

Why all this concern about the doctrinal knowledge of Lutherans? Right now, and for many years, the church has been facing challenges to its belief from the culture and even from within the church. While any organization can tolerate a certain amount of dissent, there is a limit. In a classroom a good teacher can handle one bully and still effectively teach the class. But if there are three or four bullies in a class of twenty-five, they will rule the day. If a church is too heavily populated with members who don't know the difference between Lutheranism and, say, the Congregational Church or the Church of the Brethren, then that church can easily be overcome by heresy. You have to know what you believe to know when those beliefs are being eroded, ignored or violated. We don't have to know what every other church and religion believes. That is neither possible nor necessary. But we need to know very well what *we* believe. Knowing that, we know when we hear something contrary to it.

Some terms that are common among us Lutherans can provide an abbreviated explanation of the ideas that characterize

Lutheran theology. The first and most important is **justification by faith alone**. This is what started it all. Martin Luther's personal struggle with trying to please God, trying to obey His laws perfectly, became desperate. That was what led him to the gospel's promise. In the book of Romans, these words finally penetrated Luther: "For in the gospel a righteousness from God is revealed, a righteousness that is by faith from first to last, just as it is written: 'The righteous will live by faith.'" (Romans 1:17 – NIV) A similar verse in Galatians says: "So we, too, put our faith in Christ Jesus that we may be justified by faith in Christ and not by observing the law, because by observing the law no one will be justified." (Galatians 2:16b – NIV) For Luther, it was heaven's door opened to him, an epiphany that colored his whole life, and ultimately the life of the whole Christian church.

Luther's agony at his own weaknesses, his own sins, may seem exaggerated to us, but any honest and thoughtful person knows his own failings. A friend of mine once asked, "Why is it that we are all so afraid that if our friends *really* knew us, they wouldn't like us?" It is the universal fear of the human heart. It illustrates the problem each man has when he compares what he is and does with what he knows (or thinks) God expects of him. It is impossible to satisfy the law's (God's, morality's) demands. What Luther finally saw in Romans was that of course he couldn't, but he didn't have to. In fact, the good news of scripture is that God tells us faith in Him *is* righteousness. Luther came to see the good news of reassurance throughout the Old and New Testaments, which, he said, both contain *gospel*, good news. Historically, students at Lutheran seminaries are trained in **discerning law and gospel**, that is, identifying and separating law and gospel in all of scripture, for (this may be news to some) the understanding that we are saved, or made righteous by faith is a theme of the Old Testament as well as the New Testament.

The doctrine of justification by faith alone, and not by works, (or even a combination of faith and works) is not "natural" to us. Even though we know and are uneasy about our own failings, we continue to act as if doing good now and then somehow might make up for the evils large and small that we inevitably do. Our pride gets in the way for one thing, and our desire to appear respectable. The doctrine of justification by faith alone is a doctrine of our complete and total dependence on God. Nothing we can do can possibly earn for us the right to be called righteous. We cannot fool God, or impress God or coerce God. He says *No* at every turn. Instead, He speaks the eternal *Yes* to us. "Yes, I have done it for you."

The fallout from that doctrine is great, as we shall see.

If we are saved by faith alone, and not by adherence to the law, is there any purpose anymore for the law? St. Paul asked the same question in Romans. Luther tells us that the law is not our starting place. We start with Christ, and we don't make Christ into a Moses, a law-giver. Christ is not *just* a teacher or *just* a good example. He is *the Christ,* the Messiah, the one who died on the cross and rose again *for us.*

The cross. It is not Christ *on* the cross that is central to our faith. Everybody dies. It is the *empty* cross that is central to our faith—and the empty tomb. The Romans crucified Jesus Christ, and the Jewish leaders agreed to it because Christ claimed to be one with God, God's son, God. He claimed over-lordship of everything! That's what neither the Romans nor the Jews could abide. And that would have been the end of it if he had just died. But he did not. Inconvenient for those who sentenced him. He rose again with a real body, spent six weeks walking around, eating with his apostles, coming and going among them in closed rooms and on public roads, and then was taken up right before their eyes. That was the victory. He had been accused, condemned and executed and still He returned, gloriously, victoriously *alive*. That was the proof, the dramatic demonstration that Jesus Christ is truly who he claims to be—lord of the universe. He is Lord even over death. Everything follows from that. He said that if we have faith in him we will be saved. Has anyone before had the right to say that without being laughed out of town?

That is what a Christian believes—that Jesus is *the Christ,* the Messiah, the Savior, truly God and truly Man. He is the One who has the power to redeem us, to make us righteous. This is the belief that defines the Christian, the Lutheran Christian as well as any other. If you don't believe that, even if you believe in the Golden Rule and follow the Ten Commandments and think the Sermon on the Mount is a perfect guide for life, you are not a Christian. You may be a *cultural* Christian, meaning that you live in a more or less Christian society and you try to abide by a more or less Christian morality, but you are not a member of the body of Christ.

With that understanding, we come again to law. If Jesus Christ is Lord of all, as we believe, creator, sustainer, ruler, then it follows that *His law* is the governing principle. If you made the place, if you own it all, even the people, you get to make the rules by which it all functions.

Here we have some very basic Lutheran doctrine. Since mankind rebelled against God, in Adam's fall, we are all naturally sinful. Sometimes that condition is called *original sin.* It simply means we were born of sinful parents into a world full of sinners, and an inclination to sin is universal among us. Scripture describes our condition in many ways. We are inclined to go our own way. We are a stiff-necked people. No one is perfect, not one. And so on.

God addresses that condition with *law,* which is intended to restrain evil. Its purpose is also to provide for peace and harmony here on earth. The law is God's gift to a fallen world. This law recognizes that we need rules in order to get along with each other and provides for the good of all people as they rub along together in families, communities, nations. Luther calls this **the first use of the law.**

When we are confronted with the law, when we make honest attempts to obey it, then we see our own weaknesses. As we strive to obey it, the law shows us our sinful nature; it proves to us that we can't possibly live up to it. That, says Luther, is exactly what it is meant to do. In our acknowledgement of our helplessness we are met, not by the demands of a just God, but by the unlimited love of a God who fulfills the demands of the law Himself, as we repent and have faith in His promise. That is what Lutherans call **the second use of the law—to drive us to Christ**, where we have both certainty and freedom. "This is the reason our theology is certain: it snatches us away from ourselves and places us outside ourselves, so that we do not depend on our own strength, conscience, experience, person or works but depend on that which is outside ourselves, that is, on the promise and truth of God, which cannot deceive." (Luther's Works 26:387)

When Luther spoke of these two uses of the law, he spoke of them as operating in **two kingdoms** —the left-hand, or civil kingdom where civil righteousness applies, the arena within which we live with family and neighbor, and the right-hand or spiritual kingdom where God shows us our need for him.

So in the civil realm, Christians and others live in a fallen world where they must make judgments. Here we follow Romans 13:10, which reminds us that love sums up the law, and love does no harm. So when we make decisions about the lawfulness or the morality of a particular course of action, we ask what possible harm the various choices may do. What are the consequences?. What are the damages? We decide what course to take, what remedies, based on the best wisdom and information, including Holy Scripture, and we reason. It is consistent with this use of the law that a nation might well elect to go to war, if the consequences of *not* doing so would cause more harm (in our best judgment) than the consequences of doing so. In the world, in the civil realm, the choices are not always between *right* and *wrong*. Sometimes they are between *bad* and *worse.* We must often choose the lesser of two or more evils. This particularly Lutheran understanding of the nature of the law, this first use of the law, gives us a pattern for making decisions—not an easy pattern, but a realistic one.

As we live in this way, in the world, with the best intentions to live according to God's will, we discover daily, as Luther did, the impossibility of living in perfect obedience and harmony with God. So the second use of the law takes over, and we daily, even moment by moment, repent and cry to our Lord Jesus for forgiveness. The Holy Spirit moves us to do so, and gives us faith that God *will* forgive, as indeed He does. Again and again. And He calls us righteous.

Are we therefore sinless from that moment on? Are we "sanctified", in the language of some denominations? Lutheran Christianity is a lot more realistic than that. Of course we sin again. We are still fallen and imperfect humans. That is our *condition.* At the same time it is the *condition* of God that He is always loving, always forgiving, always redeeming. For the Christian, a new *condition* takes over. Now we are not just sinners, we are **saints and sinners at the same time.** More important, it is the Christian life. That is another basic Lutheran understanding—that all of us who believe, all who are in the body of Christ are always saints (that is, righteous in God's sight) and always sinners (for we are in our very natures inclined to sin). Luther often quoted Isaiah 64:6: "All our righteous deeds are filthy rags." Not our bad deeds, mind you. Our *righteous* ones.

Scripture is central to our belief. **We believe that God speaks to us through His Word.** We believe He inspired its writing, and that through that Word, the Holy Spirit awakens faith in our hearts. He gives us faith. In his explanation of the third article of the Apostles Creed, Luther teaches that I "cannot by my own reason or strength come to Him", emphasizing that our faith is a gift from God. Another word we use for *faith* is *trust.* We count on Him, we trust in His promises.

Like Luther himself, who read the scripture through twice each year, we place great emphasis on reading the Word. We understand that when the Word is preached, it is God speaking through the speaker. We believe it is alive. Without the Word, Luther said, people "will believe anything". We have plenty of evidence today of the truth of that! The Word, in Lutheran circles, is understood to be a *spoken* Word. Preaching is, by definition, preaching of the Word.

Lutherans understand that the Bible contains books of many different kinds—poetry, history, hymns, law, narrative tales, biography, genealogy and so on. And we think some books of the Bible are weightier, more useful, than others. Luther famously said that the three most important books of the Bible are John's gospel, Romans and the first letter of Peter. The least valuable, "the epistle of straw" is James, according to Luther. Luther also said that, if he had to choose, he would give up all the stories of Christ's miracles and works in favor of His *teachings.* Classic Lutheran theology does not hold with either literal interpretation of all of scripture (treating scripture as we would a modern science text, for example) or with "proof-texting" (using a particular phrase or portion of scripture to "prove" a point). On the other hand, Luther emphasized that we should accept the most obvious meaning of any text, and not twist or ignore scripture or try to make it say what we want it to say rather than what it clearly says. That is a warning to us about some of the recent methods of interpreting scripture.

Our primary aim in reading the Word is *understanding.*

Historically, Lutherans are readers and students of the Word. We say we are saved by Grace alone, through Faith alone in the Word alone—the *solas.* It was by reading the Bible and "beating against it until it yields refreshing water as Moses beat the rock," that Luther's theology shifted, and he found the answer he was looking for, in Romans. In the Word. Luther himself came to faith through the Word.

Some of the things God says to us in His Word are going to be mysteries. "Now we see but a poor reflection, as in a mirror; then we shall see face to face, says St. Paul. (I Cor. 13:12 – NIV). But if we are to see at all, it will be through the Word.

All of us are saved in the same way, we believe, and we all receive the same gift of grace. All believers, then, belong to a **priesthood of all believers.** Luther said that God makes us so in Holy Baptism. This is a very important concept for Lutherans. Sometimes Lutherans explain the effect of our common priesthood by saying it means we can go directly to God in prayer, without the necessity of some (other) priest to intercede for us. This is an idea that has become common to most Protestants. It is one of the key differences in the popular mind between Protestants and Catholics. Luther warns that, though all Christians are priests, because God made them so, we are not all capable of "preaching, teaching and ruling". The body of Christ, any small body of believers, will select from among its members some whose vocation will be preaching, teaching and ruling. We believe those people will be called of God for that particular work. Yet we insist that the pastor or priest among us is no different, no "higher", no "more filled with grace" than any other Christian. No less. No more. From the doctrine of the priesthood of all believers, it follows that we believe there is no hierarchy of grace in God's kingdom—no priest or bishop has the authority to dispense God's grace or to withhold it, nor can he define the conditions under which it is given.

Another aspect of the priesthood is that we minister to each other. We encourage each other, pray for each other, comfort and teach each other in the faith. Together in the body, we possess all the necessary skills and abilities to appreciate each other and work together as the body of Christ, to live in this world and do the work of the church.

What then is the role of pastors among Lutherans? The pastor's special work is preaching the Word, teaching it to the people, and administering the sacraments. Our pastors are "shepherds", who concern themselves with the well-being of the flock. They are God's servants among us in a special way. At the same time, the pastor is one with the members, all equally God's children, always sinning, always forgiven, all responsible for spreading the Gospel, sharing the faith, caring for one another.

Martin Luther is himself a model for the pastoral ministry. Many of the anecdotes about him, the table talk and his warm and human sermons create a picture of a pastor who is an active preacher, concerned for the spiritual, physical and mental health of his parishioners, well-known among them. The pastor is the servant who leads. When no pastor is available, however, Lutherans believe a body of believers is still the church.

There are two sacraments in the Lutheran church, Baptism and Holy Communion, or the Lord's supper. Lutherans believe that a sacrament is a promise of God together with an earthly sign (water, wine, bread). It is an action in which the Word of God does something to and for us through an earthly element. So it is the Word and the sign. God promises to be with us "in, with, and under" the earthly sign. Through the sacraments God creates and strengthens faith in us. It is the fact that *God is acting* and that *there is an earthly element* through which He acts that makes it a sacrament. He instituted Baptism and Holy Communion; that is, He commanded that we do them. Only in Baptism and Holy Communion, those two sacraments, do we have both God's command that they be done and an earthly element as the vehicle, or sign, together with the Word, through which God acts.

God comes down to us, individually, in these sacraments.

God established the sacrament; He acts in the sacrament. We receive it. Only two sacraments satisfy those criteria. For this reason, Lutherans have only two sacraments. Roman Catholics, for example, have seven, but their understanding of what a sacrament is and does is somewhat different from ours. Lutheran theologian Gerhard O. Forde also emphasizes the *specific* and *individual* nature of the sacraments. It is "for you" individually—God acting for and in each of us, one on one. In faith, we receive the sacrament, but it is not faith that makes it valid. God makes it valid. It is faith that accepts the gift.[14]

In Baptism, the water illustrates for us that God cleanses us from sin and marks us for his own. He does it. The pastor says the words, and applies the water, but God does the acting. Baptism, as we understand it, is not the sign that a person has "made a decision for Christ". Baptism does not wait upon our decision. Baptism has nothing to do with our action or lack of action. Baptism is *God's* action. In baptism, God makes us his own. Luther is reputed to have said that he started every day by saying "I am baptized!"—reminding himself of God's action on his behalf. It is a reminder, then, of our total and utter dependence on Him, and of his total and perfect love for us.

There is no holy water in a Lutheran church. The water is ordinary water. That is the point. Through an ordinary earthly bit of matter, God in his Word makes us his children. The Word and the action go together. The water is nothing without the Word.

In Holy Communion, or the Lord's Supper, Lutherans believe that we receive Christ in the bread and the wine. The pastor or priest does not magically transform the bread or the wine into something other than what it is. As it lies on the plate or flows in the glass, the element is not in and of itself holy. But when I receive it, and when the Word is spoken, "This is my body; this is my blood" God performs an action in and for me that is as real and concrete as the elements, and as true as the Word. Lutherans believe that when I receive the bread and the wine I am truly receiving the body and blood of Jesus Christ. But, as in the water used in baptism, neither the bread nor the wine is anything but bread or wine until I receive it and the Word is spoken. We treat the communion bread and wine respectfully as we treat all things in the church respectfully, but they are still bread, still wine. The person who administers the sacrament does not change anything in the elements. Everything that happens in holy communion is God's action. That is our belief.

Neither of our sacraments is done by us for Him. Holy Communion is not our sacrifice, but His gift. In Holy Baptism, we do not dedicate a child to God; God makes a child his own. This belief about the sacraments is central to Lutheranism, and different from the beliefs held by many other denominations. It is a hallmark of Lutheran theology. This belief is being eroded among some Lutherans today. It is intricately tied to our belief that we are saved by faith alone, the Word alone, grace alone—all the work of the triune God, and not by *anything* we do.

Recently a friend mentioned that she had not taken communion lately because she so strongly disagrees with her pastor on a particular matter of the faith. At times like that, we should remember that it is not the pastor who makes the communion, and its power does not rest in the relative purity of the pastor's belief any more than it relies on the purity of one's own belief. In pioneer times in this country, occasionally it happened that a preacher came into a community for a few weeks, baptized the children, married all the couples and administered the Lord's Supper. Then he went on his way to another place. Then a rumor appeared. He was not really an ordained pastor at all! Of course everyone was angry and disappointed, but then some wise believer reminded them that all the marriages were real because the promises were made to God and the community, and the baptisms and the Lord's Supper were real because God made them so, in the elements and the Word. Too bad about the preacher.

On the strength of this belief, Lutherans have historically practiced "lay presidency"—which means "laymen presiding at baptism and holy communion." At some times and places no pastor is available. Lutherans have then selected and trained lay persons in the administration of the sacraments. As a priesthood-of-believers issue, and as a proper understanding of the nature of the sacraments, the continuation of lay presidency is a practical and proper practice which should not be taken from us. On the other hand, we do not ever participate in the Lord's Supper in a light or frivolous way. All of it, the pastor or lay person who administers the sacrament, the setting in which it occurs, the way the elements are treated, all must be done according to standards of decency and "good order"—another very Lutheran phrase.

Lutheran worship consists of the preaching of the Word and our hearing it, and the administering of the sacraments and our receiving them, and our thankful response to these gifts that God gives us. We praise God, that is, we worship Him, for what He is and for all He has done and faithfully continues to do for us and in us. When we understand our total dependence on Him and His abundant grace, when we understand our own helplessness and His eternal gifts to us, the proper response, the only response, is gratitude. Therefore, **worship consists of hearing the Word and receiving the sacrament, and responding with prayer, thanks and praise.**

In many times and places, Lutheran worship has been liturgical, very like the Catholic mass, only in the common language. We make the distinction, however, that we are not a *liturgical church,* we are a *confessional church.* It is not liturgy that defines us, but our common confession of faith. This is an important distinction. A Lutheran congregation is Lutheran by reason of its confessions, not because of the form it uses for worship.

In America, especially in the early years and in rural communities, Lutheran worship has been at times much less formal (less liturgical), including just the speaking of the Apostles Creed, a spoken confession of sin and the pastor's spoken assurance of God's forgiveness, a sermon, hymns and the Lord's prayer. There is no *required* consistent Lutheran worship pattern. However, in recent years, Lutheran hymnals have included several more elaborate liturgical settings, and Lutheran worship has in some places become nearly identical with the Roman Catholic mass. Lutheran theology does not define or require these particular forms of worship. It allows them.

A mark of Lutheran worship has traditionally been its rich musical tradition, perhaps especially its use of the music of Bach, who was a devout Lutheran. A strong choral music tradition is common among Lutherans, and the singing of hymns as entertainment on social occasions is also common. Among traditional Lutherans, it is possible to start a familiar hymn and have the whole group break into four-part harmony, *a cappella.*

Lutherans believe that Jesus Christ was truly and fully God, and at the same time truly and fully man—the only perfect man there ever was, man as God intended him to be at creation. We believe that He suffered on the cross because of our sin, that He died and rose from the dead into a new life, and that when we trust in Him we also live that **new life.** It begins here in this life as God daily pours out his grace for us, and we believe that after we die we will be raised "on the last day" just as He was, into a new life with a new body in an unending communion with Him. There will no longer be any separation between us. The sin that causes the separation will all be gone. Scripture describes this eternal life in terms such as "a new heaven and a new earth", "raised in a body like His", a life different from this in that "now we see in part; then we shall see clearly". **Eternal life is what God intended for us from the beginning.** Jesus said He came so that we could have that particular life, and lots of it—abundant life. Eternal life begins here, when we trust in God. St. Paul says "In Him we live and move and have our being." Luther said that natural life is a part of eternal life.

Lutherans have little to say about "end times" or "signs that the Lord is coming". Since we believe that eternal life begins here on earth when we trust in Christ for full, everlasting life, we are less concerned about prophecies, rapture and the like. While there are all kinds of imagery in the Bible about Heaven, and all kinds of Christian ideas about what it will be like, Lutherans don't claim to know much about the details.

In fact, Christ came to "redeem the *world"*. God intends to do something *new in the world,* not just in individuals. That "new world" will not be a replacement for this, says theologian Gerhard Forde; it will be the *fulfillment* of it, and it is going on right now.[15]

What do people *do* who are living this eternal life?

Here is one of the most wonderful descriptions of life on earth in all of Christendom. **Luther called our work on earth vocation! A calling.** The American Heritage Dictionary defines *vocation* this way:

"*A regular occupation or profession, esp. one for which a person is specially suited or qualified. An urge or predisposition to undertake a certain kind of work, esp. a religious career, calling; divine call to a religious life, a calling.*"

Luther would say "Amen!" to that, and add that every Christian's work, all of it, is his vocation—in all those senses.

Before Luther's time, the term *vocation* was used exclusively to describe one's calling to work in the church as a priest, monk or nun, for example. Luther was the first to use the term *vocation* to refer to secular offices and occupations as well.

We understand that *works* will not compensate for the evil of our sinful nature, or for any of our individual sins. Work, in the vocational sense, will not suffice either. So we are not talking about a theology of works. What *are* we talking about? We are talking about the activities of life. We are men. God made this earth, and He made us to live in it—which means, among other things, doing the work that life in the world requires and makes possible. On this earth, in God's earthly kingdom, we work. For those who believe, work takes on a new dimension. ". . .we have been released from the law so that we serve in the new way of the Spirit, and not in the old way of the written code." (Romans 7:6 – NIV) Even work is "new" in the new life we live in Christ. Luther said our work is sacred and that God takes joy in it, and blesses us through it. It becomes satisfying and fulfilling.

In the New Testament, Jesus tells us that, as long as we have light, we must do his work. (John 9:3-5 – NIV). St Paul speaks at length about the work that needs doing in the world. "There are different kinds of gifts, but the same Spirit. There are different kinds of service, but the same Lord. There are different kinds of working, but the same God works all of them in all men." (I Cor. 11:3b – NIV) All we do, we do "as for Him". The purpose of all vocations is serving others. Work is one way we love our neighbor. God's law tells us to love our neighbor. We cannot really "do" anything for God. He needs nothing. Our neighbor has needs. When our work fulfills some of those needs, it is an act of love for our neighbor. If you are able to give your neighbor a job so he can support his family, you are acting within your vocation to provide for, to act out love for your neighbor. When you do kind and compassionate things for your neighbor, those too are acts of love, vocational acts.

The Lutheran doctrine of vocation is that God calls each of us to vocations—to the good and necessary activities of life.

He said that the butcher's vocation is just as much a "calling" as the priest's. Each of us has different talents, skills, abilities and training, different strengths and weaknesses, different economic conditions. Within those opportunities and limitations, we are called to do the work of the world, and it is God's work. By going about our business as God's people we are engaged in the battle with the evils of sin, the flesh and the devil—on God's side. It is what we are intended to do. So the mother caring for her children, the teacher in the classroom, the carpenter framing a building, the engineer designing a structure, the clerk at the grocery store, the bus driver—all their work is vocation. What do we do in this world? We do His work; we pursue our vocations.

Lutheran theology is very simple. It can be summarized as a **theology of the cross.** A theology *of* the cross is very different, from a theology *about* the cross. On the cross, Christ died. His death, if it had ended there, would have been just one more piece of evidence that human life is essentially meaningless and death is its ignoble end. But an end just the same. This year's film *The Passion of the Christ* focused on that death, the violence, the excruciating pain, the brutality of it. And it was indeed horrible. Christians, when they pursue a theology *about* the cross rather than a theology *of* the cross, do not like to hear this, but it is true that other men have also suffered horrendous deaths. They say, "But His death—it was for me, for my sake, for my sins. The torture of bearing all the sin of the world puts His death in a different category." And yes, we Christians understand that His death was different in that it was *for* us. But He died. And He was buried. Like all men. Our creeds emphasize that.

But in this case, in this amazing instance, that was *not* the end of it. Friday night they wrapped his body as the Jews of the time did, and laid it in a cave, a tomb, and Caesar's governor ordered that a boulder be placed at the entrance to the tomb, and posted a guard—on a dead body! We know why. He was nervous. Yet on Sunday morning, the guards were nowhere in sight—AWOL—the boulder had been rolled aside, and the tomb was empty except for the grave clothes, which were neatly folded and lying in the tomb. That, too, might have been explained, and whole industries have devoted themselves to explaining it ever since. But still, *that* was not the end. Christ was walking around, "appearing" here and there, uncontrollably alive, eating, conversing with his friends, seen by not only his apostles, but by many others as well. That fact called *all* the explanations into question.

And what difference did it make that Christ rose from the dead? He was not a ghost or a newly dead soul visiting old haunts. He was among us *bodily.* Everything depends upon the resurrection. God came, as He said, to give us new life. The fact that He Himself died and was raised again—that He conquered death—is proof that He is capable of giving Life. We know He can because He did it, in His incarnate form. If He can do that, He can do anything. The resurrection proved that He has control of all creation, over life and over death. It proved that Jesus Christ was truly God, for only God can create out of nothing. The resurrection is both *necessary* and *sufficient* to bring the Christian life into being.

In the cross and resurrection I daily die to my old life of sin as I repent. My sinful life is crucified over and over. In the cross and resurrection of Christ I am daily born anew. I am made (created) righteous in Him—that is, His righteousness covers me, too.

When I live in the theology of the cross, I live with the reality that nothing I do is "good" in the sense of *righteous*, perfect in God's sight. As His child, as a believer, as one who has faith in Jesus Christ, my life is a constant repentance, a constant return to Him for his life-giving forgiveness. The gospel, the good news of salvation through Christ's death and resurrection on the cross, is not something I experience once and that "takes care of it" from then on. Neither do I "get saved" over and over again. The gospel is good news to the Christian every day, as he daily repents, as he is daily justified, forgiven, made righteous. In the cross.

The theology of the cross emphasizes the *alone,* in faith *alone,* grace *alone,* the Word *alone.* That is the complete sufficiency of the cross. Nothing more can be added. The architect Mies van der Rohe said (of building and "decoration") "Less is More". Christ turns that on its head. "More is Less." Anything we add, anything we require of each other, anything any church leader requires of us *in addition to the cross,* diminishes the theology of the cross.

The fact is, it happened. The fact is, because it happened, the door to new life was opened for me. The fact is, that is *all* that really matters. That is the theology of the cross.

* * *

Lutheranism may wear many faces. Its forms of worship may vary greatly. Its hymns in one place may be different from its hymns in another. But we are not defined by those forms and practices; we are defined by this body of belief. When we make changes in our programs, policies, structures, rites, we must know *why* we make the changes. They must be consistent with our beliefs, with our theology. Whatever is not of Christ, whatever diminishes the theology of the cross, whatever elevates man and demotes God, whatever whispers "works will do it" and whatever panders after the approval of our neighbors without concerning itself for God's will, all that we must reject.

And what do we get? The freedom that comes from knowing we are favorite children of a loving God, inheritors of *all* He has. All life. All righteousness. All joy. All freedom.

I Want to Do It Myself!

A little guy we know was helped out of his car seat by his grandfather while the boy screamed and struggled. Grandpa set him down on the sidewalk, and the tot turned around and promptly climbed back up into the car and fastened his seat belt. He waited for a minute, looking angrily at Grandpa. Then he unbuckled the seat belt and climbed out of the car seat, out of the car, onto the sidewalk.

"I wanted to do it myself!" he said. Firmly.

God must get tired of that line.

Nicodemus came creeping to Jesus one night to find out if He really was "from God". Jesus answered in John 3:16-20. You can only know it if you are born again of the spirit. But that wasn't enough for Nicodemus. "How can this be?" So Jesus gave Nicodemus (and us) this wonderful summary of his life and our gift: "For God so loved the world that he gave his one and only Son, that whoever believes in him shall not perish but have eternal life. For God did not send his Son into the world to condemn the world, but to save the world through him. Whoever believes in him is not condemned." (NIV.) Is that it? Is that all? We have the impression that Nicodemus was skeptical. *We're* skeptical.

It is Christ's message, though. Once we are alerted to it, we see this message repeated everywhere in scripture. Sometimes the word is *trust*, or *faith* and sometimes, as here, it is *believe.* The meaning is consistent. The Gospels relentlessly hammer home the point that Christ has saved us. Whoever believes in Christ, trusts that he *is* the Christ, that person already has salvation. He already has eternal life.

It is too easy. So we make it difficult. We ask, "Do I believe *enough?*" "What if I don't *feel* any different?" "I have to do something to deserve it, otherwise how can I hold my head up if I accept his forgiveness without doing anything?" "How can I believe it if I don't understand it?"

We have all had those thoughts. Some of us have said them out loud. Some are nagged by these nay-saying doubts for years. On the other hand, the promise is so bright that we can't entirely put it out of our minds.

Biblical literalists tell us that we can be saved if we believe in Christ *and* in the literal accuracy of every word of Scripture. Some say we can be saved if we believe *and* read the Bible every day. Some say we can be saved if we believe *and* refrain from dancing, card-playing, smoking and/or drinking. Some say we must believe *and* give time and money to the poor.

We do have trouble keeping our eye on the ball. We get distracted. We try to do good works purely out of love for God, and then we look around and see that there are others who aren't joining us in our particular good work. We are irritated with them in our hearts, and proud of ourselves in a martyr-ly way. Before long we're advocating works-righteousness. "You ought to. . ." Forgetting (how can we?) the magnificence of the promise. We forget our position, our relationship. We obey the rules of the house because they are the rules of the Ruler. We live in the house because He says we can. We may think our neighbor is not doing as good a job of living up to the rules as we are, but the Ruler tells us making that judgment is against The Rules. The Ruler says our believing neighbor—the one we look down upon, the one who embarrasses us—is our equal.

He is a full inheritor in the kingdom. Instead of being thankful for all that He gives us, we begin to point fingers at our neighbor accompanied by all varieties of "You should. . .".

We can do many things for ourselves. Achieving righteousness is not one of them. It's one thing we can never do for ourselves.

Rules and Regs

In speaking of Lutheran theology, we must necessarily spend considerable time talking about law, what it is, what it does, what it can't do, why we have it. And we repeat faithfully that adherence to Law is not cash in the bank. It won't buy you anything. We say that as if it were a totally unfamiliar idea outside of the faith, as if no child in far off Patagonia nor any heathen in the jungles of the Amazon would naturally understand it.

We're wrong about that.

Let's start at home. There are rules in our house. There were rules when the kids were young:

Don't run in the house.

You have to make your bed first thing in the morning.

Don't hit your brother.

Don't hit your sister.

If you want to fight, do it in the backyard.

Don't buy groceries on a credit card.

Don't go out without telling us where you're going and when you'll be back.

Say "I love you" at least once a day.

Wipe your feet.

Turn off the lights when you leave the room.

Flush.

Now think about it. How much credit do you get for obeying those rules? Don't you grimace when your child turns goody-goody and shines his semi-angelic face up to you saying some version of, "Haven't I been good, and aren't my sisters bad?" By comparison, you know. He wants credit for it.

It doesn't work that way. It's a wise wife or husband or child or boss who occasionally commends us for being so reliable, but we all understand it's no big deal. Being on time at work is not service beyond the call; it's properly expected. Picking up your room is not a matter of great virtue; it's a matter of being able to find stuff and keeping the place clean. Rules in our daily lives form the necessary base line.

It's the same with the laws of the land. Speeding is against the law. But you don't get three free accidents for driving forty years without getting a ticket. No one is going to pat you on the head or award you a lottery pot because you didn't kill your neighbor. And no wife is going to consider that ten years of marital faithfulness entitles you to one affair. The rewards for keeping the law amount to this: you don't get fined, put in jail or ostracized. Keeping the law is just *what is expected.* To say someone is a law-abiding citizen is very nice. But even the most law-abiding fellow in town, we all assume, is at least a little lucky. Some time or other he just didn't get caught.

These are aspects of law everybody understands. Even those who consciously break it.

So now we come to scripture, which tells us that we must obey the laws of God, but that doing so will not *earn* us anything in heaven or on earth. Is God telling us anything we don't know already? We know it. We just don't like it.

My Word!

We knit our brows about many things. Jesus once made the point with his friends that one thing is more important than the daily concerns we have—whether they be housekeeping tasks or solving whatever health crisis appears. He said 'you are worried and upset about many things, but only one thing is needed. Mary has chosen what is better, and it will not be taken away from her." Luke 10:41-42 NIV.

And what is the "better" that Mary chose? Sitting at the Lord's feet, listening to what he says. (Luke 10:39)

For many years I dreaded the Sunday when Martha and Mary were paraded in front of us, and poor old Martha (with whom I strongly identified) was put down because she complained that she was doing all the work and could sure use a little help. I, too, could sure have used a little help, especially on Sundays, getting a pair of little ones ready for church and a dinner in the oven by 8:00 AM. It was foolish to try to do it the way my mother had, but a lot of what I do is foolish. As long as I saw it in terms of how the work gets divided up, (or doesn't, as the case may be) I missed the point.

The church is perpetually in danger of taking Martha's side, too. A congregation takes on various obligations, and then it must fill in the blanks with people and hours—volunteers. "We need six people to act as greeters this Sunday, twenty-two for vacation Bible school, at least two to cook at the homeless shelter on Wednesday, a new chairman for the altar committee to arrange for communion this month, etc." Who is going to do the work? Who will help? These are necessary tasks. Like scrubbing the kitchen floor and folding the laundry, somebody needs to do this work that serves those we care for. And there is so much of it. And it never gets equitably divided. Lord, Martha had a point.

But Jesus, as always, had *the point.*

The story of Mary, Martha and our Lord zeroes right in on the day-to-day tensions of the Christian life. We live in a material world, and we are dependent for our physical well-being on the things God has created and the work we must do to make it all useable. We grow, spin, weave, sew, manufacture, distribute, sell, purchase, care for, use up, replace and ultimately discard one thing after another. We depend on the created world for the basic ingredients, but much must be done to and with them to turn them into anything useful. Beyond that, He made us in such a way that we are not satisfied with just *anything* to eat or to wear. We discover pleasures associated with these things. The smell of freshly ironed shirts and line-dried sheets. The odor of Mom's best beef burgundy stewing on the stove. Bread in the oven. The pleasure of sparkling clean windows and an orderly closet. The joy of performing a service for which we are paid. Setting a bone. Building a house. Selling the best kids' shoes in town. Solving a marketing problem. Delivering new automobiles. Managing money.

Everything in life requires work. Some of the work is sheer joy. Some is endless repetitive drudgery. In a human way it is our destiny to work. We derive pleasures from doing our work well, from solving the problems associated with our work, from achieving goals.

And still it is not enough. "What does it all mean?" we ask. "Is this it?"

God the Creator also built into us a longing, a dream of perfection, a yearning. In *The Confessions,* St. Augustine says that our hearts are restless until they rest in God.

All of this is present at the table in the house of Lazarus, Mary and Martha in Bethany.

This little anecdote of Jesus' human life, of his relationship with a particular family, is touching. He had come for dinner. Like the best dinners at my house, he had come, even more, for conversation and fellowship. The four of them (I imagine Lazarus was there too) probably had a relationship like the relationships George and I have with several folks—we like to "get together". We like to be in the same room, to enjoy eating and drinking and talking together. It enlarges us and feeds us. We like to provide the best food we can, and we do considerable work to make that possible, but in the end, we always judge the success of the event, not by how well the roast turned out, or how good the sauce was, but by how lively and good the conversation was. That was the reason for getting together.

In this case, we cannot forget, even for a moment, who Jesus is. Do you ever wonder what it might be like to have a particular famous person at your table for dinner? I should have liked a long visit with Alec Guinness or C. S. Lewis. Thomas Sowell and Walter Williams as a pair would be delightful. Blake Hurst, a farmer who writes for the American Enterprise magazine has long been a favorite of mine. The author Ferrol Sams is high on my list. With a guest like any of those, one would be very happy to just keep pouring the wine and later the coffee and port and hope to hear as much as possible of what he had to say. Don't you suppose the family at Bethany, who understood that Jesus was the Christ, wanted most of all to hear what He had to say? Even Martha, though she may have momentarily forgotten it.

Jesus said Mary had chosen the *better* part. It is always a matter of priorities, isn't it? He is saying to me, here, that the most important thing, the first thing always, is hearing the Word.

Jesus said Mary chose the better part—to listen to Him. We spend a lot of time in the church, appropriately, studying and listening to the Word. Why do we do that? Here it is. See the arrows pointing here from all directions. Hear the crescendo of the orchestra. **The Word is central because that is where we learn of God. That is where we hear His promise. The words of scripture are the words the Holy Spirit speaks to us. It is in and through the Word that the Holy Spirit whispers to us, and finally shouts. And it is within that process that the triune God bestows faith.** He who has ears to hear, let him hear the good news.

The gospel, the incredible amazing good news that is the gospel, is God's promise to us. He promises us that he has already atoned for our sinfulness and our sins. A vow. Just like a marriage. The marriage metaphor is perfect. Christ the groom takes a bride—the church—the whole body of believers, as his own. Christ the groom, claims the bride; he brings all the gifts; he endows his bride with all he has—himself. He is central. Mary's focus on him, and on hearing what he has to say—that is the response Jesus is looking for.

As the bride of Christ, what then should be central in the church? The Word. Of course. He is the Word. The Word was before anything was. The Word is Truth. The Word demands a hearer. "If a tree falls in the forest and no one hears it fall. . ." So what? But if the Word of God is spoken and no one hears it, the silence is lethal. Worse yet, if the hearers are gathered with their ears washed out and their eyes wide open and no one speaks the Word, will the church fall down?

"So", says Mary, "who will do the work?"

A World Full of Feelings

Goethe said "Feeling is all there is." Damn Goethe. Excuse me. Some in the ELCA agree with him.

It is a problem that has been with us for a long time, this elevation of "feeling", and its attendant devaluation of *thinking.* Consider what it does to us, this notion that feeling, if it isn't all, it is at least the most important thing.

For some time, at the outdoor flower-child weddings we attended in the '70s and '80s, couples who wrote their own vows were inclined to promise each other to be faithful "as long as we both shall *love".* Cute. The "honest" admission that we two probably won't always feel as we do now, so we're marrying with our eyes wide open. Even Johnny Carson said that it is hard to get excited about those limited vows. To love one another forever—that means something. To love as long as it feels good; well, it lacks a certain something. We don't hear that so much at weddings lately, but I sense that the sentiment lies under it anyway. We've formed calluses on that subject. The wedding is lavish. The honeymoon is to die for. The marriage lasts three years. But there's no point in going on if it just doesn't feel good anymore.

We have tender feelings. Your neighbor's little girl is a terror. She has taken to biting. You don't want your children to play with her anymore, but you're afraid to tell the mother. It might hurt her feelings.

Feeling is everything so we have to make every sacrifice (at least *somebody* makes every sacrifice) to protect the feelings of those about us. We think it is our Christian duty. We think that's what love is.

Then there's the matter of "having a feeling about something". Intuition can be valuable, but if so it's usually based on some real information or experience. We're not talking about that. We're talking about the employee who just has a feeling that his new co-worker looks down on him and wants the boss to move him into another position. Or the young woman who goes to the Tarot card reader. "It just makes me feel good about my decisions when the cards confirm them. I don't really make my decisions based on that, you know—I just like to be easy in my mind about them."

We also hear a fair amount of "I want to feel good about what I do." "I clean the highway because it makes me feel good." "I want to be a nurse so I can feel good about how I earn a living." The so-called service professions are elevated above work like shoe repair, farming, construction, truck driving. It's all about feeling. It's very nice to get good feelings whenever they occur. Making good feelings one's aim is a poor goal.

If such incidents make your eyes cross, good for you. There's a chance your brain cells are still viable.

What happens when "feeling" hits the church? Facing the fact that we sin does not make us feel good. I have heard more than one person say that he has left the church because he just couldn't stand all that guilt. If the church is preaching a theology of guilt and works righteousness and penance on top of it, okay. A church seeker will be better off somewhere else. But not to assuage his feelings! If he is just trying to escape the hard truth—we all sin—then he will also be escaping the promise of the gospel. God can forgive sin.

In the church we place all our hope on faith. Isn't faith a feeling? Don't we just have to abandon our reason when we seek God? It appears that is what some folks think. Belief is all about emotion; it requires abandoning reason. Is that so? Are all of those who believe stupid? Or uneducated? Or weak? In a play on Broadway this spring Tom Stoppard puts these words in the mouth of one of the characters: "Atheism is a crutch for those who can't face the reality of God." A nice twist on the notion that faith is a crutch. Faith is not a feeling. It is a gift. It may generate feelings, but in itself, no, faith is not a feeling.

I cannot prove that God exists, or that Christ's death and resurrection cancels my sin. Nor can I prove that there is no God, or that Christ died and that is the end of it. It takes as much "faith" to live a life of "NO" to God as it does to live a life open to Him. But we can reason a long way toward faith. My faith is, in fact, based on reason, as was St. Paul's, and St. Augustine's and that of every Christian who has ever lived—even those who saw and lived with the Lord Jesus. We still have to weigh what we know with what is claimed. C. S. Lewis said "The battle is between faith and reason on one side and emotion and imagination on the other." (*Mere Christianity*, Book III, Chapter 11.) This is the problem of the ages.

Perhaps there have always been churches and Christians who played the "feelings card" rather than the reason card. Conversion can be a tremendously emotional event. It must have been for St. Paul. We know it was for Martin Luther. Some of us have had similar experiences. In our life as Christians there are times when inexplicable emotion overwhelms us. I had such an emotional dream once, and it caused me to make an important change in my life. I have also experienced the inexplicable peace and safety of my Lord in a time of great stress. These are gifts. The test of faith, however, comes on ordinary flat days.

There's an old English proverb:

It's not the 'opping over 'edges that breaks the 'orses' 'ooves;
It's the 'ammer, 'ammer, 'ammer on the 'ard 'ighway.

What did St. Paul do after his encounter with Jesus Christ on the road to Damascus? He tells us in Galatians 1:17-18 NIV. "I went immediately into Arabia and later returned to Damascus. Then after three years, I went up to Jerusalem to get acquainted with Peter and stayed with him fifteen days." He got on the road. He did a lot of walking and a lot of preaching, and some visiting and consulting. As far as we know, Christ never struck him down again. It was one foot in front of the other from then on. There were certainly emotional experiences along the way, not all of them pleasant. But Paul did not live on the emotion. He couldn't have done the work he did if he depended on some kind of emotional high from the Lord every day.

Here is the danger of a religion dependent on feeling. We can't create it; we can't depend upon it; we can't make it last.

There are churches and Christians who thrive on emotion. Some of them appear to be very successful. Should we emulate them? Should our sermons evoke tears? Should our hymns always make us blissfully, if temporarily, happy? Should our prayers always transport us to a place of perfect peace? What place do thought or study or self-examination or repentance or trust in the face of adversity have in the Church of Good Feelings? Should we serve feeling and sensation over thought or conviction or principle?

After the honeymoon, the real acts of love make the marriage. After the leap of faith, the daily walk takes us the rest of the way. Tears and laughter no extra charge.

Good Work(s)

Is doing "good works" different from "doing good work?" It is a useful question to contemplate.

Luther was addressing that question *exactly* when he said that all our work is *vocation,* the butcher's work as much as the priest's. It is interesting that in Germany in recent years (and I am assuming also in Luther's time) the butcher's work was held in low regard in the culture, as in our culture the used car salesman and the ditch digger are cultural symbols of work that is beneath respectable citizens. Why would Luther use such an extreme example to make his point? Other than the fact that Luther seems to have enjoyed extreme expressions.

The Christian knows that law and work are somehow related. Both concern *what we do.* In the Christian faith, we understand that law and work are related through *love.* In Romans 13, St. Paul tells us that loving our neighbor as we love ourselves is the summation of the law. (It's not the only place, or even the first place, we read that in scripture.) And St. Paul goes on to say that love cannot do harm to the neighbor, therefore the whole of the law is summed up in love.

Love, as the term is consistently used in scripture, is an active verb, or as a noun, it is the name of an action. Love is action. It is act. That is a very important understanding for our time, when the culture is screaming that love is a feeling. Marriages dissolve for lack of "feeling". Causes expire because they are difficult to "empathize with". A culture of victims plays on public emotion to arouse sympathy and special treatment. We justify our irresponsibility and our lack of perseverance on the basis of a lack of "satisfaction". Conversely, we accord greater honor to acts which people do that we imagine produce no good feeling in the doer.

All of those attitudes wander away from reality; that is, away from the fact that love manifests itself in action or it isn't love at all. Feeling sorry that your child is hungry isn't going to help him. The act of feeding him is the love that is required. The provider for the family, when he works for pay to provide for his family's needs, is doing a daily, repeated act of love. The family that acts out its appreciation for those gifts, is also acting out love.

Love gets more complicated when we operate as an organization, specifically as the organization we call the church. The church undertakes various works, contracts to provide services and support for the spiritual and material well-being of its members and others in the community and the world. It provides, in church language "opportunities for service." So far so good.

But inside the blink of an eye, the church labels those particular acts, giving our time and money in the church and to the church and its programs "works for the Lord", or even "good works". As opposed to what?

Is there a difference between *vocation* and *good work?* Or even *good works?* The beautiful six-panel oak door the cabinet maker builds—that sterling example of excellent workmanship—is that good work, but not yet *a good work*, as in a *work done to the glory of God*? Is such workmanship worthy of faint praise only? Is it only the poor evidence of an inferior vocation?

The church as an organization and some of its pastors and even some of us who are "the workers" are often guilty of making such judgments. It is subtle, but powerful. Do we speak as often in glowing terms of what a great doctor John is, or what a reliable and skillful electrician Gene is, or what an excellent business woman Laurie is—do we say that with the same intensity, the same appreciation, the same esteem that we say how faithful Mark, the church janitor is, or how much we depend upon Ashley when it comes time to help a bride prepare her wedding, or what a faithful visitor to shut-ins Carl is? What message are we sending about work? What are we teaching about the nature of love?

In the even wider sphere, we in the church need to consider the question whether our activities truly act out love to our neighbors. How do we know? We measure the consequences. Love does not do harm to the neighbor. We are responsible to evaluate our own actions in the light of that word.

That means, among other things, that we measure our acts by their results. Do the poor and the homeless and the hungry whom we help become self-sufficient as a result of our help? Or do they become dependent on it, and less able to make their way productively in the world? We must not, as governments so often do, measure our success in the numbers of people who ask for our help. We must measure it, if it is love, in the numbers who receive help that moves them out of the doldrums of "have not" into the world of having and doing.

We must be as wise as the canniest businessman, and as savvy as the street cop who's seen it all. We are not called to be naïve do-gooders, but *effective* lovers, doing effective work.

That is a call to the church to be students of economics and government, to be realistic and optimistic at the same time. Realistic, because we know how often our efforts fail, how slow we are to learn, how many mistakes we make, no matter what we try to do. Optimistic, because we are doing what we are called to do. Optimistic because we serve the Lord who taught us the value of the one sheep that was lost, the one coin that was missing.

So we return, as we always must, to the cross. We will fail. It may take us two dozen tries and five years to develop a product that fulfills a particular need and does it reliably. We may start six businesses before one succeeds. We may preach the word every Sunday and wait for years to be surprised at one who heard it. Love does not harm its neighbor. And it may not bring great rewards to the doer, or it may bring them very late. That's why one of the cardinal virtues is perseverance. When we fail, as inevitably we do, we evaluate our failures, we ask forgiveness for them, and in that grace, in that forgiveness, we are given the freedom to keep on doing our vocations.

Good work is a big order. But I don't have to do it all alone. I couldn't anyway. So within all the work of the world, my particular vocations, my particular callings, fulfill some of the needs of the world. Someone else, many someones, fulfill the others. We do our own work as to the Lord, and we appreciate the work others do in the same cause, and we leave it to the Lord Jesus to make the final judgments.

WHAT IF?

What if? Two words. The keys to all creativity. What if I impale this chunk of meat on a stick and hold it above the fire? Maybe it won't burn on the edges so fast. What if horses were red and blue? Wouldn't that look great in a golden pasture? What if I dug a trench from this river over here to the place where the barley grows? What if you and I rubbed our noses together?

Creativity is not harmless, of course. Someone must have asked, "What if we flew a commercial jet into the World Trade Center?" Everything in the world needs redemption, even creativity.

God apparently creates all the time. He is the Creator. That's what He does. I am made in His image, a shadow, at this stage, of Him. My husband is at his most creative in the shower. Often enough to be funny, he comes roaring out of the shower with the answer to a problem (related to deep foundations, probably), talking it through as he dresses. I get my best ideas as I come out of sleep early in the morning, which makes me very poor company at breakfast and is the chief cause of breakfast dishes left undone till noon.

This morning it hit me. What if we opened the morning

paper to this headline (on page two, obviously): **Church Headquarters Mysteriously Disappear.** The article goes on to say that

> *Late last night in Chicago a dense fog descended on Higgins Road. It was impossible to see six inches for about twenty minutes. Then a tornado-like wind roared in, dispersed the fog and left—nothing! No parking lot. No buildings. Nothing. Reports have come in from around the country that a similar event occurred in 65 locations around the country. Office buildings, in some cases just two floors of a building, disappeared, leaving strange voids in the structures. There are reports that home computers and briefcases containing materials related to the church's activities have also disappeared. "It's very confusing," said the secretary to a bishop in Omaha. "We don't appear to have any records at all. And I can't remember anything we've done for the last ten years! I don't know how we are going to recoup this loss." The presiding bishop has been hospitalized with a minor case of heart palpitation, but is expected to be released this morning. Reporters around the country are interviewing pastors of local churches for the human interest side of the story.*

A follow-up story appears in the Religion section on Saturday.

> *Pastor Marvin Olander of Foothills Lutheran Church reports that church services will go on as scheduled tomorrow morning at 8:30 and 11:00 with Sunday School at the usual 9:45 hour. "Really, nothing much has changed around here," says Pastor Olander. "My associate Pastor Susan Marshall spent about an hour Wednesday morning on the phone to find out what she could. Apparently the whole superstructure of the church has disappeared." When asked what has happened to the people who worked at the various headquarters, Pastor Olander replied that there has been a shortage of pastors in the church for some time, and he understands that some of the bishops and staff pas-*

tors have been approached by congregations to serve as parish pastors. "It would solve one of the problems the church has had recently," he said. And what about the various missions and programs of the church? "We're not sure yet how that's going to shake out. It's kind of exciting, really. We've been talking with some other churches in town as well as a few of our sister churches around the country. Our church council is reviewing our benevolence budget next week. We're confident we can continue all the important things."

What if it really happened?

Bureaucracy has grown tremendously in the church. "Program" has grown. The more agencies and committees we have, the more "issues" we address, the more people involve themselves in management, direction, and "services" for the congregations, the less we concentrate on preaching and celebrating Jesus Christ.

When our family first started camping, when the children were little, we got a tent trailer and outfitted it for three-week jaunts. The thing that amazed me the most (other than the mosquitoes and the dirt) was how few things we actually needed to eat, sleep, keep warm and entertain ourselves. At home we had a whole house and closets and cupboards full of stuff. In camp we managed most of the same activities with a few clothes, a minimal cook kit, a portable stove and some sleeping bags. Oh, and matches and an axe. The big plus was that, with so little to organize and keep clean, we had lots more time to hike and visit interesting places, to read, to sit around the campfire and talk, to be a family.

We are back to living in a house, of course. And glad of it. But I have never looked at "stuff" in the same way. Keeping things simple, even in a relative way, is a necessary part of life. We pull the weeds so the beans can grow. We pass on the outgrown clothing so we have room for trousers that fit. We try to keep dustables to a minimum. Why? It's not just aesthetic. It's so we have time for the important things. We try to limit our commitments so we can do well the things we promise to do. It is our aim (not always realized) to mind our own business as much as possible. We know what is best for us; we trust (we try to) that our children and our neighbors know what is best for them.

What if the church learned those lessons?

Bureaucracy in all denominations has become a problem. Several books on the subject are appearing. Many of the problems in the ELCA today are of our own making. If we had "just said no" to the historic episcopate, for example, we wouldn't have spent all that time and money meeting and propagandizing and defending the CCM, and all the organizations that have arisen (and also cost money) to oppose it, might have been spending those dollars to promote the gospel and do the work of loving our neighbors. All the men and women who spent so many hours in meetings over that subject could have been playing tennis, fishing with the kids, buying flowers for their wives, and cleaning the closets instead.

This "what if" stuff is addictive.

Is the ELCA Lutheran?

It's not a stupid question.

We are one body of *the church—the church, one, holy, catholic and apostolic.* It could be said that its beginning is described in Acts 1:6-8: "So when they met together, they asked him, 'Lord, are you at this time going to restore the kingdom of Israel?' He said to them: 'It is not for you to know the time or dates the Father has set by his own authority. But you will receive power when the Holy Spirit comes on you; and you will be my witnesses in Jerusalem, and in all of Judea and Samaria, and to the ends of the earth.'" (NIV). When He said this, Jesus was with the apostles He had chosen. There were eleven left, and after saying this, He was taken up to heaven as they watched. Shortly after, they selected a twelfth apostle by lot.

Jesus was leaving them. He was sending the Holy Spirit, so He would continue to be with them, but in a certain sense, from now on they were on their own. He had left open the question about restoring the kingdom of Israel. They would come to understand that in time. Starting from that time, about 30 AD, and from that place, Jerusalem, the apostles would spread out and bring the Word to the known world. Saul of Tarsus would be added to their number later, and would become the "apostle to the Gentiles". If we accept this as the beginning of the church, we are agreeing that the church is everywhere they went, and everywhere the Word was carried and has gone since, where the gospel has been and continues to be preached, and where the Holy Spirit breathes faith into any heart.

The church in this largest sense is *for all time.* On All Saints Day we sometimes sing hymns like "Behold A Host", emphasizing that we here on earth are one with our brothers and sisters who have gone before. All those who have ever believed are part of that great congregation. The church is also *everywhere.* It is in Uganda where the influence of the Christian church is making successful inroads against the AIDS epidemic in Africa—the only nation where that is happening at this moment. It is alive and well in Malaysia, where Chinese Christian immigrants' children are the engineers and teachers and businessmen in an otherwise Muslim country. It is alive in Niwot, Colorado, where a new Christian church is planted magnificently in the middle of a parking lot nearly always full. And the church is *various.* Open the yellow pages of any telephone book, even in a community as small as Moscow, Idaho, and be amazed at the number of different headings. In my community of around 200,000, there are fifty-four headings for churches, and that does not count the Buddist, Islam and Jewish headings. Three of those headings are Lutheran: ELCA, Missouri and Wisconsin synods.

We are a part of that larger church which transcends space and time, and we must keep that in mind. We are one of many Christian bodies, naturally and legitimately most intimately concerned with this one part of the whole body of Christ of which we are a part, the ELCA. We know the basics of our theology and our history. Most of us know *the church* as the congregation we belong to now, and those we have belonged to over our lifetimes. Some of us know first-hand the workings of the church on the synod and national level. Most of us do not.

We all know the story of the man who gets to make all the big decisions and his wife makes the little ones. He decides whether we should go to war, and she decides what house to buy, how many children they'll have, what they will eat and who will be their friends. Like his wife, we in the congregations are faced with a smaller, more important, more difficult decisions. We need information to make those decisions.

What is gathered here is just what an interested layman can piece together from the newspapers, the internet, conversations with others, articles in Lutheran publications, e-mail, and publications of various reform movements within the church. The mission of the church of Christ is to bring to each person who is born the good news of the gospel. The ELCA is only one small vehicle of that mission. On the other hand, it is *our particular vehicle.*

Our particular vehicle. Is it what it ought to be? Are we who our confessions say we are?

To answer the question "is the ELCA Lutheran?" we compare what the ELCA does and says with the confessional beliefs we hold as Lutherans. Lutheran beliefs hang together. Because we believe in the priesthood of believers, we all receive, equally, the grace of our Lord. We all take on the tasks and responsibilities properly belonging to a priestly body. Because we believe that we are justified by faith in Jesus Christ and nothing else, we keep an eye out for the "extra somethings" imposed on us, by ourselves and by others. Because we believe that the death and resurrection of Jesus Christ is everything we need for our salvation and it is enough, we don't try to embellish or change it. Within this faith we are given the fullness of Christ's salvation, the abundance of eternal life.

Do we still believe that? Do our leaders and their staffs believe it?

It seems clear from the evidence where the ELCA leadership is heading. It is clear, given the way the ELCA elects its leaders and makes policy decisions, that the membership of the ELCA cannot change the leadership without the concerted efforts of a huge majority in each synod and among the bishops and all the synod committees.

It is also evident that the church is already split. Unfortunately, and perfectly predictably, it is split right down every congregation and inside many families. Those of us who are unhappy with the direction the church is taking will be called divisive. We will be called that for simply pointing out that things are not as they seem. We will be called that for being the messengers bringing bad news.

The bad news, the really bad news, is that sooner or later real decisions will have to be made by pastors, congregations, or, failing that, by individuals. Lutherans who know what it means to be Lutherans will want to be in congregations that are unquestionably Lutheran.

In an important sense, it does not matter what happens at Church Wide Assembly in 2005. If they vote to ordain non-celibate homosexuals and officially bless same sex unions in some way, nothing will have changed. Both of those activities are going on within the church right now. If the vote is for "local option"—decisions church by church—*lots* of decisions will have to be made. And it will be obvious that they will have to be made over and over and over wherever a congregation says *no*. If the CWA votes against ordination for non-celibate homosexuals and/or against blessing same sex unions, the 2007 Church Wide Assembly will be voting on those issues again. And perhaps even again. That is the pattern of the GLBT lobby as well as the pattern of the church leadership in issues they want passed. Remember how the ELCA-ECUSA agreement was finally voted in.

Nothing will happen dramatically. All the same options are

on the table that have been there since the founding of the ELCA. Individuals and congregations can withhold benevolence and see what happens. So far, nothing much has happened as a result of the decline in giving. The ELCA headquarters is tightening its budget and laying off some people. No policies have changed, and no programs have been dropped.

The number of congregations joining WordAlone Network and/or Lutheran Congregations in Mission for Christ will continue to grow, perhaps at an increased pace. Your congregation may decide to be among them.

Individual members of congregations will move to new congregations in the great ELCA shuffle that has been going on for a long time. Other individuals will leave the ELCA entirely, and some will no longer attend any Lutheran church. Some will go to other denominations; some will go to no church anymore.

Meanwhile, the ECUSA steamroller is close behind. How long before all our pastors are ordained "with episcopal orders"? How long before lay presidency fades away? How long before we have bishops ordained "for life"? How long before we quit talking about justification by faith *alone?* How long before *the priesthood of all believers* becomes just an archaic phrase?

No decision, of course, *is* a decision.

One of my pastors tells us often that the opposite of *love* is not *hate.* It is *indifference.* If we love our church, if we love the Lutheran faith, can we ignore the ELCA leadership and just continue to "do our own thing"? If these issues matter, how are we going to respond? Will we be indifferent?

Up Close and Personal

Today I can say (and I do say) without hesitation that the ELCA is a bust. It appears that it never was truly a union of Lutheran bodies—not one that worked. It bears all the marks of a botched job, a hastily arranged marriage in which each of the parties (the LCA and the ALC) was hoping that the other would change and become, magically, the partner the other longed for. Potential problems lurked in every corner. Everybody tried to pretend that they could easily be resolved once the merger was accomplished, ignoring the fact that any one of those problems was already a festering canker that had proved persistent and troublesome. The more one thinks of it in terms of a marriage the clearer this becomes. From the beginning, the "democratic process" in which the merger was born was hedged and managed in the diversity representation mode that passes these days for correct (if not honest) democratic involvement. Quotas were introduced into the church structure very early in the process, and they continue to provide a focus that diverts attention from far more important matters. Add to that the fact that the leaders of the ALC and the LCA during the process were hesitant and skeptical (the parents didn't favor the marriage). The homosexual issue had already reared its head and was not dealt with. The issue of authority of scripture was not settled convincingly, an amazing weakness considering the history of the Lutheran church. The issue of lay presidency (a priesthood-of-all-believers issue if there ever was one) was not resolved and troubles us to this day. Congregational centrality, though lip service was given to it during the negotiations, suffered greatly. The issues of who owns church property, who "controls" the pastoral call process, how the layman is represented in the church at large, the relative emphases of evangelism and social action—all of these dog us still.

Churches are hard to move. I know this from personal experience as well as from anecdotal and historical evidence. There are many reasons for this, and they all work against the best interests of earnest believers.

The first reason is the benign ignorance of most of us laymen in our congregations. Those of us who are committed Christians are inclined to say that we are Christians first, and Lutherans second. Or we say we are Christian by choice and Lutheran by the accident of birth, marriage or geographical proximity. There is usually some truth in it when we say that. But there is a huge problem with that attitude. It assumes that whether one is a Lutheran or a Baptist or a Unitarian or a member of the Church of Christ is immaterial. The ecumenical movement has fed heartily on that notion, and what has it produced? A watered-down and puny American Christianity.

Luther emphasized the importance of knowing doctrine. He said every Christian should be so well educated in the faith that he is sure of his faith and doctrine, so as to be able to defend his faith against all comers. If we are Lutherans, at the very least we should know what Lutherans believe. We do not need to know all the details of what every Christian denomination believes. That would be impossible anyway. But we do need to know what the basics of Lutheran theology (our doctrine) are. We need to know them well enough to defend them first to ourselves. The chapter *What Lutherans Believe* in this book attempts to set out Lutheran belief in concise understandable terms. Lutherans should be familiar with Luther's Small Catechism and be constant serious students of the Bible. Does your church teach these things to its young confirmands? Are they emphasized and explained in your congregation's new member classes? When someone joins your church, can you be confident that he knows what it means to be saved by faith alone, awakened by the Holy Spirit through the Word alone, a trust in God's amazing grace alone? Does he or she know what we mean when we say we are not saved by our works, but by faith? Does he think it means that it doesn't matter what we do, or how we live? How does God's law enter in to this picture? What doctrines does your pastor believe and preach? We dare not be ignorant of doctrine, or we stand in danger of losing the reason for our church's existence. It's that important. And yet it is possible to attend many Lutheran churches week after week and be ignorant of our doctrine. That is the first deplorable ignorance.

There are many in our congregations who are *social* Christians—nice likeable people who go to church out of habit, because it is a thing good people do—who are relatively unmoved by the claims and promises of the Gospel. A vital, doctrinally faithful church witnesses to those folks weekly, even daily, confident that through the preaching of the word and the administration of the sacraments the Holy Spirit will work in those hearts, too. If we do not constantly educate (preach and teach the word) we cannot claim to be the witnessing, ministering church we were commissioned to be.

We are ignorant also of the workings of our denomination. This is a more forgivable ignorance, perhaps. Denominational structures, workings and politics are like housekeeping. As someone once said of government and housekeeping, as long as things are going along well we don't notice them. It's when they fail that they suddenly become important. In the church we begin to notice when we discover that there is a shortage of pastors, that there is an even worse shortage of good pastors. We notice when newspaper articles appear saying things about Lutherans that sound very foreign to us. We notice when an issue arises (such as the ordination of non-celibate pastors who have declared that they are homosexual) and we discover that we have no effective direct way to address the issue. How many of us know what the ELCA Church Council is, when it meets and what it does? What do we know of the workings of our own geographical synods? What do we know of the seminary training our pastors are getting today? And what of the educational materials that are coming out of our church headquarters? Today, for those who have not noticed, we have to educate ourselves about these things, for all is definitely not well in any of these areas.

So ignorance is at the heart of the immovability of Lutheran congregations. Loyalty and sentimentality are the two other interrelated impediments to necessary reform in the church. Never mind that the preaching is bland and thin on content. Never mind that there is no Bible study for adults. Never mind that membership is declining. Never mind that the church has begun to talk of baptism in suspiciously magical terms. My children were baptized here. My grandfather and grandmother were married here. I know the man who designed the stained glass window over the altar, and I participated in the bake sale that raised the money to have it made. What would Christmas be like without the choir singing at the eleven o'clock service and all the lights out and just candles glowing in the windows? Think of all the fun we have at the annual church picnic and the fall harvest banquet. Why, the men's club has done all the repairs around here for years, and the bishop is the son of a family friend in Iowa. It is no good making fun of these ties. There is not one among us who is not conservative and sentimental in his heart. We have made a life. Church is a part of it. The people, the places, the memories. If we question too much, we may weaken those ties. It is all too frightening.

It takes a great deal to shake people enough to turn their backs on a church or a denomination to which they have belonged—the word is crucial—to which they have *belonged*—for many years.

It isn't nice. It may even be immoral. We have names for people who leave the congregation. They are church-shoppers. They are disloyal. They are trouble-makers. They are divisive. We have seen them before. When we meet them by accident at the grocer or in the mall, we are uncomfortable. We try to be nice, of course, but we don't want to talk about it with them. Better to be dismissively friendly and scurry back home. And we certainly don't want to be such people ourselves.

No matter what.

It should be no surprise, then, that no matter what goes wrong in a church, no matter how unhappy one may be, no matter if the church's most basic doctrine is being challenged or even discarded, a faithful member is likely to hang on for a very long unhappy time.

This sounds like the words of someone who has given up and is looking back both angrily and nostalgically. It's true. When I began the book, I planned a section on hope. There is no such section here. Is there any hope?

We are commanded, however, to hope. Faith, hope and love abide. How many Israelites on their way to Babylon discovered soul-mates among the refugee lines? How many, when they got there, came together in communities of faith more vital than any they had known before? As the ELCA continues in its chosen path, here and there faithful Lutherans are finding each other. Perhaps that is where our hope lies.

Resources for Further Study

Websites

affirms.org. Site dedicated to affirming Lutheranism. They believe that Called to Common Mission is "null and void". Source of information about CCM, its meaning, consequences, etc. Aimed at ELCA Lutherans. Discussion groups, polling, membership information.

alpb.org. American Lutheran Publicity Bureau. Inter-Lutheran independent organization. Promotes Lutheran confessional belief. Publishes books, tracts, music, newsletter, etc. Useful website.

elca.org. Evangelical Lutheran Church in America. Very useful website of the ELCA. Many layers of information. Note especially "Messages from the Presiding Bishop". An excellent way to keep up with what the ELCA is doing. Just a little savvy reading between the lines will reveal what the ELCA's direction and theology are.

doradocovenant.org. A covenant written by several ELCA pastors of large churches affirming traditional marriage, etc. Website provides an opportunity to sign the covenant, which will be presented to the Presiding Bishop.

elcf.net. The Evangelical Lutheran Confessing Fellowship.

"Embraces" the Lutheran confessions. Posts news articles related to ELCA and its activities. See particularly "Open Letter" under "News" for an eye-opening description of ELCA headquarters. ELCF promotes the activities of Communities of Grace.

lcmc.net. Lutheran Congregations in Mission for Christ. An alternative and/or a companion organization to the ELCA. Website describes the organization, contains whole text of its constitution and by-laws, its mission statement, congregations (113 in Oct. 2004) who are associated with LCMC, information on joining. LCMC offers a viable alternative to the ELCA for congregations that wish to remain Lutheran and do not believe they can do that within the ELCA. Joint ELCA/LCMC membership is permitted. Pastoral ordination, pastoral referrals, management of pension funds and health benefits are available through LCMC.

lcna.org. Lutherans Concern/North America. "A Christian ministry affirming God's love for people of all sexual orientations." Works for ordination of GLBT people. Not a reorientation organization.

reformation.com. A collection of news reports of ministers of all denominations sexually abusing children. Names, denominations, details of charges.

sldrc.org. Solid Rock Lutherans. "To call the Evangelical Lutheran Church in America to remain faithful to the Word of God according to the Lutheran Confessions." Currently working to secure delegates to the 2005 Church Wide Assembly who will vote against proposed changes in ELCA policy regarding same-sex unions and celibacy for all single rostered persons in the ELCA. Some good material on the "Journeying

Together Faithfully" ELCA study on the homosexuality issues.

snapnetwork.org. Survivors Network of those Abused by Priests. Begun, as the name suggests, in response to the scandal in the Roman Catholic Church. Includes all denominations today. Suicide hot line. Book reviews. Press releases. Support groups. Speakers bureau.

soulforce.org. Organization promoting the interests and acceptance of gay, lesbian, bi-sexual and transgender people. Promotes direct action (sit-ins, passing out leaflets, marches, etc.). Is organizing for the 2005 Church Wide Assembly in Orlando.

wordalone.org. Website of the WordAlone Network. Very useful and interesting site. Contains texts of addresses to WA conventions and conferences, press releases, lists of congregational members, information about WA activities, helpful study materials, etc. WordAlone is a major player in the reform movement within the ELCA.

PERIODICAL PUBLICATIONS.

First Things. Ten issues per year. Scholarly and timely articles about conservative Christian issues with emphasis on issues in the public arena. Published by the Institute on Religion and Public Life, 156 Fifth Ave., New York, NY 10010. $34 per year. Website: http://www.firstthings.com.

Forum Letter. Monthly publication of the American Lutheran Publicity Bureau, and

Lutheran Forum, a quarterly journal. Reports events in Lutheran bodies, theological deliberation, etc. Solid commentary on current events in all the Lutheran bodies. Subscriptions (for both publications) $24.95 per year. Available overseas for $7.50 additional. Individual copies: $2.50. American Lutheran Publicity Bureau, P.O. Box 327, Delhi, NY 13753-0327.

Lutheran Commentator. Bi-monthly newsletter published by Lutheran Commentator, a Minnesota non-profit corporation. Excellent up-to-the-minute news about ELCA activities. Analysis of issues, on-going theological information and discussion. Issues oriented. Reliable source of real information with dates, places, names, etc. Subscriptions from Lutheran Commentator, P.O. Box 103, Maple Plain, MN 555359-0103. $12 per year, $22 two years, $30 three years. $10 students and seniors.

Lutheran Quarterly. A scholarly and interesting journal, containing articles discussing "the Lutheran faith and life on the basis of the Lutheran confessions, for the application of the principles of the Lutheran church to the changing problems of religion and society, for the fostering of world Lutheranism, and for the promotion of understanding between Lutheran and other Christians." Subscriptions $30 per year, $55 two years. From Lutheran Quarterly, S. 2715 Ray St., Spokane, WA 99223, or 1-800-555-3813.

Touchstone: A Journal of Mere Christianity. Interdenominational publication, "conservative in doctrine and eclectic in content, with editors and readers fsrom each of the three great divisions of Christendom—Protestant, Catholic and Orthodox". Interesting and timely articles. For the general Christian reader. Published by The Fellowship of St. James. Subscriptions from *Touchstone* Subscription Services, P.O. Box 3000, Denville, NJ 07834. $29.95 per year, $49.95 two years. Website: www.touchstonemag.com.

BOOKS

The following books are helpful in understanding the ELCA, Lutheran theology and history, and issues before the church today.

Anatomy of a Merger by Edgar Trexler. Augsburg, Minneapolis, 1989. The cleverest thing about it is the title. A fascinating account of the process by which several Lutheran bodies became the one ELCA written by an "insider". From our viewpoint today, Trexler's book shows us the seeds of many of today's problems in the ELCA. Interesting for people who are fascinated by organizations and how they work.

Christian Sexuality: Normative and Pastoral Principles, edited by Russell E. Saltzman. Kirk House Publishers, Minneapolis; and ALPB Books, Delhi, NY., 2003. Nine essays on the subject by speakers who participated in a conference held in Kansas City in October 2002. An excellent collection by acknowledged experts. Very helpful for those who are concerned with sexuality issues within the context of Christian orthodoxy and compassion.

The Church and Homosexuality: Searching for a Middle Ground by Merton P. Strommen. Kirk House Publishers, Minneapolis, 2001. Merton P. Strommen's credentials are impeccable. He is both an ELCA pastor and a research psychologist, a Fellow in the American Psychological Association. It is no puzzle that the ELCA is not promoting his work actively, but it's a great shame that they are not, for his work demonstrates both a scientific approach to understanding homosexuality and the compassion of a Christian pastor. A short, readable, useful book.

Faith and Freedom: An Invitation to the Writings of Martin Luther edited by John F. Thornton and Susan B. Varenne. Vintage Spiritual Classics, Vintage Books, a Division of Random House, Inc., NY, 2002. There are many books of Luther's writings—he wrote so much. This is just one, but a good one to start with. The Lutheran faith as it was taught by Luther himself is timely, helpful and inspiring today. Always good reading, never esoteric; Luther speaks clearly to all of us "ordinary" Christians.

Here I Stand by Roland Bainton. The most popular biography, and the modern standard before Kittleson's. Very good reading.

A History of Lutheranism by Eric W. Gritsch. Fortress Press, Minneapolis, 2002. A history that is fascinating, all-encompassing and enjoyable to read. While it is not a theological work, it is useful in understanding how Lutherans came to be what and who they are.

Luther the Reformer: The Story of the Man and His Career by James M. Kittelson. Augsburg Publishing House, Minneapolis, 1986. An excellent and very readable biography of Martin Luther, with maps and a good index. I put this at the top of the list for understand Luther and the church of his time.

Where God Meets Man: Luther's Down-to-Earth Approach to the Gospel by Gerhard O Forde. Augsburg Publishing House, Minneapolis, 1972. I purchased a used copy of this little (128pp) book some time ago, and I can't believe anyone let it go. My copy is now well highlighted and underlined. He makes the Lutheran faith come alive in all its warmth and promise. I can't recommend it too highly, and that goes for other books by Forde as well.

A DVD/VHS

Homosexuality: Perspectives for the Church from NEW CREATION: Lutheran Marriage and Family Advocates, P.O. Box 390535, Minneapolis, MN 55439. $30.00 for either the DVD or VHS format plus $8.00 shipping and handling. Visa or Mastercard accepted. Four "perspectives" on homosexuality—from a pastor, from a former lesbian, from a Lutheran Theologian, and from Dr. Strommen, an ELCA pastor and practicing psychologist. This is an excellent video presentation to share with your friends and family.

Organizations, Petitions, Etc.

WordAlone Network

The mission statement of the WordAlone Network:

WordAlone is a Lutheran grassroots network of congregations and individuals committed to the authority of the Word manifest in Jesus the Christ as proclaimed in Scripture and safeguarded through the work of the Holy Spirit. WordAlone advocates reform and renewal of the church, representative governance, theological integrity, and freedom from a mandated historic episcopate.

While WordAlone came together in response to the ELCA-ECUSA ecumenical agreement, *Called to Common Mission (CCM),* the CCM itself was not, is not, the reason for

WordAlone's existence. According to Director Pastor Mark Chavez, the CCM was merely the catalyst. People all over the ELCA, pastors, theologians and laymen alike, were troubled about many things in the ELCA, and had been for some time. The CCM was just one of the many symptoms that all is not well in the ELCA. The WordAlone Network brought many of those concerned folks together. Today, after the passage of the CCM, the WordAlone continues to advocate for freedom for seminarians to choose *not* to be ordained within the historic episcopate. In 2002, the WordAlone convened an international Lutheran theological forum to produce a statement, an *admonition*, addressing the issue of a mandatory historic episcopate within the confessional framework of Lutheran doctrine. (The Admonition follows.) The hope and intent is that the ELCA will eventually adopt the Admonition.

Since then, the WordAlone has approved a statement on sex and marriage, which also follows this entry.

WordAlone is supported by individuals who join, receive the Network News, and may attend the annual convention in April and the annual fall conference. WordAlone encourages and facilitates the formation of *chapters*—local associations of WordAlone congregations and individuals who meet for information, study and support. While individual membership is useful, association with a chapter is more helpful. The staff at the WordAlone offices are very helpful to congregations who may consider forming chapters.

Support may be the most important thing WordAlone provides. Pastor Mark Chavez says that WordAlone members, when they talk about the Network with people who have never heard about it, are often met with tears and the statement: "I thought I was the only one!" Through association with WordAlone, individuals and congregations may find the comfort and strength of association with others of a like mind—no small thing.

WordAlone also maintains *Clergy Connect*, a clearinghouse for congregations seeking pastors who believe "that Christ alone is sufficient for the unity of the Church and that the Word of God is the authority for the Church:"

WordAlone in its public meetings does a terrific job of addressing ELCA issues within a framework of joyous and inspirational worship. A WordAlone conference is a marvelous experience. That is to say, WordAlone is not a bunch of cranks who sit around and complain. It is an association of dedicated, energetic, well-informed Christians that feels like the church to which you always wanted to belong.

Find WordAlone on its website www.wordalone.org. E-mail correspondence may be addressed to: wordalone@popp.net. By phone, 651-633-4260 or 888-551-7254. FAX no.: 651-633-4260. By regular mail: 2299 Palmer Drive, Suite 220; New Brighton, MN 55112.

WordAlone is a nonprofit 501(c)(3) corporation. Contributions are fully tax-deductible, and always welcome. Through these contributions WordAlone helps seminarians pay off seminary debt, funds conferences and conventions, pays travel and other expenses for a theological advisory board, produces a bimonthly newsletter, and maintains the necessary organization and staff to facilitate and coordinate these efforts. Among other things.

LUTHERAN CONGREGATIONS IN MISSION FOR CHRIST (LCMC)

Lutheran Congregations in Mission for Christ is an outgrowth of the WordAlone Network. In its first year, the WordAlone Network board drafted the first constitution for LCMC. The constitution was adopted and 25 congregations became charter members of LCMC in March of 2001 in Phoenix, Arizona. Their mission statement says that they are:

An association of congregations and individuals who are free in Christ, accountable to one another, rooted in the Scriptures and Lutheran Confessions, working together to fulfill Christ's Great Commission to go and make disciples of all nations.

Congregations that wish to associate with LCMC may remain also in the ELCA; LCMC has no restrictions against that. However, some leaders of the ELCA are working to ban the practice. LCMC allows for the formation of "districts"—loose associations between congregations in LCMC—which may be either geographical or non-geographical in nature. Any LCMC congregation may belong to one or more districts, or none. That is up to the congregation. Districts have no legislative authority in the association. The purpose of the districts is to engage in cooperative efforts to fulfill the Great Commission.

LCMC provides an excellent pension and benefits program for its church employees. It has a reciprocity agreement with the Board of Pensions of the ELCA which allows the transfer of pension funds from the ELCA plan to the LCMC plan for members who leave the rosters of the ELCA.

LCMC is recognized as an official Lutheran church body by the ELCA which removes any property issues for congregations that leave the ELCA to associate with LCMC.

Congregations interested in LCMC may go to the LCMC website, www.lcmc.org, to find answers to questions about its constitution, membership, history, etc. There are 120 LCMC congregations to date (October 2004) in 26 states and 3 countries. Rev. Bill Sullivan, LCMC's National Service Coordinator, spends much of his time visiting congregations who want to learn more about LCMC and are interested in joining.

Two people constitute the entire paid staff of LCMC. Their Board of Directors are all volunteers.

LCMC hold annual gatherings.

Bill Sullivan may be contacted by phone at 734-207-5400, FAX 734-459-2311, or by mail at LCMC, 7000 N. Sheldon Road, Canton, MI 48187. Sullivan's e-mail: wsullivan@ameritech.net. Director of Operations, Sharon MacFayden's e-mail: lcmcadmin@sbcglobal.net.

Appendix A
Resolutions Currently Circulating

Admonition for the Sake of the True Peace and Unity of the Church

November 18, 2002

(The WordAlone Network's Theological Advisory Board held their first meeting November 16-18, 2002 in Mahtomedi, Minn. This group of international Lutheran theologians issued an admonition to the Evangelical Lutheran Church in America.)

I. Theological Foundation

Jesus Christ, our God and Lord, "was handed over to death for our trespasses and was raised for our justification" (Rom. 4:25, cf., Smalcald Articles II.1). We affirm together that we are justified by grace alone, that is, by faith alone through Christ alone. This comes about through the Holy Spirit by means of the gospel alone in its two forms of proclamation and sacrament. Whereas through the law God convicts, through the gospel God forgives, and raises the sinner unto new life. This is a life free from law, sin and death, and at the same time, rich in fruits of the new obedience.

The church of Christ is the communion of saints, that is, the communion of believers, the communion of those who are justified sinners. That means the church comes into being in the same way and at the same time with faith and justification: through the Holy Spirit by the proclamation of the gospel and the distribution of the sacraments. These two forms of the gospel, and only these, are the means through which the church is created and sustained; they and only they make the church apostolic; they and only they make the church catholic; they and only they make the church holy; they and only they make the church one. By them, and only by them, the church, its apostolicity, its catholicity, its holiness, and its unity is unequivocally made manifest.

As the creature of the gospel and communion of the believers, the church is called to proclaim the gospel which brings about justification. This ministry is divinely instituted and bestowed by God upon the whole church (Augsburg Confession 5). It is the responsibility of all believers to participate in it and to propagate the good news where they find themselves in life. For this purpose, the Holy Spirit graces the church and invests the gifts of that grace in all believers. To preach and administer the sacraments publicly in the name of the church is the specific calling of the ordained ministry (Augsburg Confession 14). Ordination does not confer any quality or special ability higher than that bestowed in baptism. Ordination is the call to proclaim the divine word entrusted to all publicly on behalf of the whole church.

There are many other elements and features which belong

to the church, like worship, loving service for the world, discipline, and oversight. The church cannot be without them. But how they are shaped and lived out is dependent on circumstances, history and cultural background. Their specific shape is neither something that makes the church the church, nor that by which the church is recognized. In other words, their specific shape is necessary neither for justification, nor for the church to be the church. In this respect, their specific shaping is indifferent (*adiaphoron*).

Since what makes the church the church, and what makes it one, holy, catholic and apostolic, and is sufficient for this, is the pure proclamation of the gospel and the right administration of the sacraments, none of those elements which are indifferent as regards justification and the being of the church can be made necessary for its unity (Augsburg Confession 7). Therefore, it is wrong "when anyone imposes such ceremonies, commands, and prescriptions upon the community of God with coercive force as if they were necessary, against its Christian freedom, which it has in external matters" (*Formula of Concord,* Epitome, Article X). The distinction between that which is necessary and that which is not necessary in the church must be absolutely clear, both in the teaching and practice of the church. If any "indifferent" element is made a condition for the being, the apostolicity or the unity of the church, this distinction is blurred. Thus Christian freedom, which is an essential dimension of the Christian faith, is destroyed, and the Lordship of Jesus Christ over His Church is compromised.

II. Ecclesial Consequences

In 1999 the Churchwide Assembly of the Evangelical Lutheran Church in America (ELCA), in order to enter into full communion with the Episcopal Church USA, mandated on a churchwide scale episcopal succession and ordination by bishops for the sake of unity. It seems clear that the ELCA, by accepting these practices as a condition of unity, has made an *adiaphoron* into a theological necessity, thus contradicting its own confessional basis. What intimates that this might not be so is the by-law amendment (ELCA Constitution 7.31.17) allowing presbyteral ordination. In order to ensure that an *adiaphoron* has not been made a theological necessity, however, what is now an exception must be made an option of equal standing. Likewise the two practices of installing bishops, with or without the participation of (three) bishops in episcopal succession, must be options of equal standing

Therefore, we ask the ELCA to amend its constitution and by-laws accordingly so that the constitution is brought back in line with its own confessional basis. Although this might be a difficult process, it is necessary for the sake of the truth of the gospel and the church's true peace and unity: "For weakening this article and forcing human commands upon the church as if they were necessary . . . already paves the way to idolatry" (*Formula of Concord,* Solid Declaration X).

Drafted and Signed by:

Dr. James Bangsund, Senior Lecturer, Old Testament and Hebrew, Makumira University College, Tanzania

Dr. James Burtness, Emeritus Professor of Systematic Theology, Luther Seminary, St. Paul, Minnesota

Dr. Gerhard Forde, Emeritus Professor of Systematic Theology, Luther Seminary, St. Paul, Minnesota

Dr. George W. Forell, Carver Distinguished Professor Emeritus, University of Iowa, Iowa City, Iowa

Dr. Roy A. Harrisville, Emeritus Professor of New Testament, Luther Seminary, St. Paul, Minnesota

Dr. Jack Dean Kingsbury, Emeritus Professor of New Testament, Union Theological Seminary, Richmond, Virginia

Dr. James Nestingen, Professor of Church History, Luther Seminary, St. Paul, Minnesota

Dr. Steven D. Paulson, Associate Professor of Systematic Theology, Luther Seminary, St. Paul, Minnesota

Dr. Hans Schwarz, Professor of Systematic Theology and Contemporary Theological Issues, University of Regensburg, Germany

Dr. Walter Sundberg, Professor of Church History, Luther Seminary, St. Paul, Minnesota

Dr. Martin Synnes, Associate Professor of New Testament, The Norwegian Lutheran School of Theology (Det Teologiske Menighetsfakultet), Oslo, Norway

Dr. Dorothea Wendebourg, Professor of Church History, Humboldt University, Berlin, Germany

Dr. Vitor Westhelle, Professor of Systematic Theology, Lutheran School of Theology in Chicago, Illinois

Also signed by:

Dr. Mary Jane Haemig, Associate Professor of Church History, Luther Seminary, St. Paul, Minnesota

Dr. Gerhard Krodel, Emeritus Professor of New Testament, Lutheran Theological Seminary at Gettysburg, Pennsylvania

Dr. Gottfried Krodel, Emeritus Professor of Church History, Valparaiso University, Indiana

Marriage and Family Resolution

From WordAlone Network

The Marriage and Family Group, a committee of seven laypersons and pastors, which is studying the Biblical and confessional understanding of God's gifts of marriage and the family, is offering a sample resolution supporting earlier stands on human sexuality and ordination standards.

The resolution, first offered at WordAlone Network's 2002 convention, can be used by congregations to let their synods know how they feel about human sexuality and homosexuality issues being studied by the Evangelical Lutheran Church in America (ELCA) for the next three years.

WHEREAS these churchwide studies are exploring the specific issues of (a) blessing same-sex unions and (b) ordaining gay and lesbian persons living in committed relationships, and

WHEREAS the Confession of Faith of the ELCA commits this church to regarding the canonical Scriptures of the Old and New Testaments as "the inspired Word of God and the authoritative source and norm of its proclamation, faith and life" and the Lutheran Confessions as "further valid interpretations of the faith of the Church,"

THEREFORE, BE IT RESOLVED that the ______________________ affirms and endorses as a faithful expression of biblical and confessional teaching regarding the question of blessing same-sex unions, those statements regarding human sexuality and homosexual behavior already adopted by the Evangelical Lutheran Church in America, to wit, the statement of the October 1993 meeting of the ELCA Conference of Bishops, that

> *"[T]here is basis neither in Scripture nor tradition for the establishment of an official ceremony by this church for the blessing of a homosexual relationship. We, therefore, do not approve such a ceremony as an official action of this church's ministry;"*

and, as a faithful expression of biblical and confessional teaching regarding sexual conduct of ELCA pastors and particularly the question of ordaining gay and lesbian persons in committed relationships, the statement contained within the 1990 ELCA Church Council document *Vision and Expectations*, that

> *"[T]he expectations of this church regarding the sexual conduct of its ordained ministers are grounded in the understanding that human sexuality is a gift from God and that ordained ministers are to live in such a way as to honor this gift. Ordained ministers are expected to reject sexual promiscuity, the manipulation of others for purposes of sexual gratification, and all attempts of sexual seduction and sexual harassment, including taking physical or emotional advantage of others. Single ordained ministers are expected to live a chaste life.*

> *Married ordained ministers are expected to live in fidelity to their spouses, giving expression to sexual intimacy within a marriage relationship that is mutual, chaste, and faithful. Ordained ministers who are homosexual in their self-understanding are expected to abstain from homosexual sexual relationships;"* and

BE IT FURTHER RESOLVED that the ____________________affirms the following statements of biblical and confessional principles of the Lutheran Church in support of the previous actions of the ELCA, and as a guide to the deliberations of the ELCA committee guiding the churchwide studies on human sexuality and homosexuality:

We believe, teach and confess that

1. Sexuality is a good gift God graciously bestows on humanity for the sake of love, devotion, and procreation.

2. By creating us male and female, God has built gender complementarity into the very fabric of human existence.

3. Marriage, the lifelong union of fidelity between one man and one woman, is the only relationship God has ordained for the full expression of human sexuality.

4. Marriage is neither a private arrangement nor merely a human construct or custom. It is, rather, a divine institution by which God has founded human community "in a joy that begins now and is brought to perfection in the life to come." (LBW, p. 203)

5. Neither the scriptures nor the Lutheran Confessions grant any authorization to the church to recognize as divinely approved any relationship other than the marriage of one man and one woman for the full expression of human sexuality; and

BE IT FURTHER RESOLVED that the ____________________ memorializes the _____ Churchwide Assembly of the Evangelical Lutheran Church in America to affirm these scriptural and confessional principles regarding human sexuality and homosexual behavior and to adopt no changes in its teaching or practice that contradict these principles.

Appendix B

The Church I Grew Up In

Who are we? What does it mean to say "I am a Lutheran?" How are we different from other Christians? How are we alike? What events and influences made us what we are? If we are going to defend the Lutheran faith, the Lutheran church, we should know what we fight for.

History is, in part, the recollections and anecdotes of people who lived it. The stories that follow are just that—stories, memories, impressions of people from all across America and one from Germany. They give us pictures of congregations, pastors, and young members of Lutheran churches. What were they taught? What do they remember? What impressions do they carry with them of their early years in the church?

The people interviewed all grew up in Lutheran churches, and all are still members of Lutheran churches today. Most of them are part of the great mobile society that is America—they moved away from their childhood home at some time. Some of them have moved many times. A few still worship in the churches and among the people of their childhood. They come from several "branches" of Lutheranism. No attempt was made to present, through these interviews, a comprehensive view of Lutheran churches. Still, some idea of the great variety and the wonderful human peculiarity comes through.

Beaver Valley Lutheran Church
Valley Springs, South Dakota

I grew up in a country church in rural South Dakota in the years 1935-1957. The church was formed in 1873 by a seminary student from Rock Island, Illinois. He came to our part of the Dakotas for a visit, and finding no church there, he married several of the couples who had set up housekeeping together, baptized their children and preached. When he finished seminary, he returned to establish a church there. The folk in the community were mostly Swedes, and they naturally thought to start a Lutheran church, but as it grew, the pastor and others felt that they wanted a more pietistic thrust, and the pastor tried to get the church to ally itself with the Swedish Evangelical Covenant Church. It never came to a vote, but it was clear that many agreed with him, and so they and he left and formed the Swedone Evangelical Covenant Church of Rock Island, Illinois, and Beaver Valley Lutheran allied itself with the Augustana Synod of the Lutheran church. When I was growing up, the membership was about three hundred and fifty, all middle class farmers and a few of their city relatives. Today the church has a thousand members. The city of Sioux Falls has grown and Beaver Valley is no longer in the country, but sits among suburban houses on large acreages. I have not been a member there for nearly fifty years, but I visit often when I go home to see my parents and family members.

The preaching at Beaver Valley was always excellent, even scholarly. The occasional complaint was that the sermons were too long, that is, more than forty-five minutes. Some folks also wanted to introduce more "modern" hymns—that is Nineteenth Century hymns. That was probably a desire for more evangelical hymns, with more evangelical texts. The first pastor I remember was an excellent preacher and directed the choir as well. Beaver Valley always had an excellent music program. Our preachers were well-trained theologians, serious students of scripture; they knew the scriptures backwards and forwards. In confirmation, we used Luther's Small Catechism and Tanner's workbook to go with it. We had to memorize thirty Bible verses which the pastor would test us on by calling out the citation, and we had to come up with the verse. I never doubted the validity of the Scriptural witness. We were fallen, saved through the sacrifice of Jesus, God's only Son. I learned to live in grace through the witness of that church. There was never any doubt, either, that sin continued to live in our lives, nor any doubt that we could be forgiven. Repentance, *turning around*, was emphasized, and that has been a part of my life ever since.

Most of us went to church because our parents, grandparents and in some cases great-grandparents went there. Our church was relatively pietistic. From a layman's point of view, that meant that the people were concerned about their conduct. They wanted to act in such a way that both in church and in the secular world, it would be known that they were believers. We had wonderful pastors who were well loved, and the spiritual life of the church became the life lived by most of us. In our small parish, the pastors generally visited often in members' homes. The Sunday afternoon call by the pastor was commonplace in my early life, but that slowed and eventually stopped because of World War II. Almost everyone in the church was Lutheran from his baptism, so we never thought about the possibility that there might be some other theology.

Today's Lutheran churches differ in that they tend to deemphasize the second use of the law—to drive sinners to God for forgiveness. Most of us in my first church were very familiar with that use. The third use of the law, to provide a model for the Christian life, was emphasized in a moderately pietistic way, but it was not a major emphasis. Today's church seems most concerned about "fitting in" to society. I hear very little law, and very little meaningful Gospel today. Rather, I hear the church (*ergo*, the people) needing to be a part of the culture in order to bring the message of love to the world. That's not what Lutheranism is about. Unitarians have done that, but not Lutherans. Our concern is with bringing the message of salvation to the world. Lutherans have always said that without the cross, the suffering and death of Jesus, there can be no salvation. Mel Gibson's "The Passion" is being panned by all kinds of people (many of whom have not seen it), yet believers come away from it fearfully convicted of the burden their sins placed on Jesus. I don't hear that at all in my Lutheran church today.

Theologically and homiletically, we're very different from the church of my youth, and I think that's a giant step backward. Ceremony has become the most important part of worship. My first church used a quite formal liturgy, modeled after that of the Church of Sweden, but it became routinized, and we never thought much about it. People think a lot about ceremony today, and I think it's silly. An interesting aside, I invited a college friend to a vespers service at my church once, and he commented afterwards that he hadn't expected to hear an opera in church.

Probably the church is better today in that we are not as ethnically and economically exclusive as we once were. That is a bit of a conundrum though. The Missouri Synod, for example, has done very well with its mission to black Americans in the South. It may be easier for pastors to preach meaningfully to a more homogenous congregation. It may be easier to serve such a congregation in all ways. Attempts to diversify, unless they occur naturally in response to gradual demographic changes in a congregation, are usually unsuccessful. I don't know the answer to this.

Evangelical Kirche
Karlsbad, Czechoslovakia

My first church was the Evangelical Church of Karlsbad, Czechoslovakia where I lived from 1933-1946, except for a year in 1938-39 when we lived in Leipzig and attended St Thomas Church. (The Lutheran church is called the *Evangelische* in contrast to *Katolische* in Germany.) I have no idea how large the congregation in Karlsband was, but the town was mostly (perhaps 95%) Catholic.

Karlsbad was a thriving city. In and around Karlsbad porcelain and crystal of high quality were produced; the kaolin was even mined nearby. Jewelers, furriers, tailors and others catered to the cultured and wealthy folk who came to Karlsbad's famous spas. Many people earned a living in the hotels and restaurants that also served the travelers. In the surrounding countryside, a varied agriculture flourished, including the growing of hops for the breweries in town. And then, of course there were the shopkeepers and tradesmen that a lively town needs. The members of the Evangelical congregation were mostly Germans and some Austrians, and the fact that they were there probably explains the presence of an Evangelical church at all in that Catholic area.

I lived with my grandparents, who were Catholics. I was baptized in the Evangelical church but I often attended the Catholic Church with them. The Evangelical church was simpler architecturally and the interior was more austere than the Catholic church.

I don't remember anything about the preaching. What I

remember is the one hour class each week when our school was dismissed and we went to separate classrooms for religious instruction. There we learned the Ten Commandments and heard simple Bible stories. At first the pastor taught the class, but when the war started the pastors were called into the army and then lay people took over the classes. In those classes I learned about good and evil. Of course I learned about God and being a Christian at home, too. My grandparents were very devout. Grandfather knelt beside his bed every night and prayed before he slept. Grandmother prayed in her chair.

Every one worked hard. Grandfather had a butcher shop and he worked six days a week, but on Sunday afternoons we went for walks in the woods sometimes. There were places along the path where a cross or a grotto was placed, and the older folks would stop there and pray. I was impatient of course. I wanted to run and play.

When we went to church, it was a solemn and holy business. People were quiet and concentrated on the service. There was no social life at the church that I knew of. I think people took it all more seriously. My mother and grandmother always made the sign of the cross and blessed the bread before they cut it. We prayed before all our meals. In general, people were freer about showing their faith—crossing themselves, praying with others, etc. I think we are more nonchalant now. We have less respect for the holy. Church worship services, however, are very much the same now as then.

By the time I was of confirmation age, we had moved to Wallau an der Lahn in Hessen. If you know Germany, Hessen is the region that includes Wiesbaden. I went to the Lutheran (Evangelical) church for catechism classes. It is interesting that, though my grandparents were Catholic and my parents were Lutheran, there was no conflict about religion in our home. My grandparents were glad to have me take catechism classes in the Evangelical church. I was confirmed there.

After the war, I went into military service with the West German border patrol. We had no chaplains, and going to church was definitely not *macho*. I never went. After emigrating to the U.S. and marrying, my wife and I began attending a Lutheran mission church that met at first in a school gymnasium. As I've grown older, my faith has grown.

I still like decorum and dignity in a church service. I have to see a cross there. The most important things in church for me are good preaching and good Bible study.

First Lutheran Church
Ontario, California

Prince of Peace Church
Montclair, California

When I was six years old my family moved to Ontario, California, about forty miles east of Los Angeles. California was growing very rapidly in those days. We joined the First Lutheran Church in Ontario. It was wonderful. The pastor was a remarkable man, very well educated, a good preacher. His sermons were intelligent, scholarly, even brilliant. He and his wife had three daughters. The older two were twins about my age and we were friends. All of the girls were smart and pretty and popular. Their whole family was admirable and we all liked them and looked up to them.

That was the church I was confirmed in. In 1959, shortly after my confirmation, First Lutheran started a mission church in nearby Montclair. My parents were among the First Lutheran members who decided to help form the mission church, Prince of Peace. Since I had been recently confirmed, my name appears among the charter members along with the names of my parents and others.

Not too long after that, First Lutheran was hit by scandal. It came out that our well-loved and much-admired pastor was an alcoholic. I don't know any of the details of how it came to light, or exactly what the church did about it, but he did leave the church. (Those were not things our parents ever spoke of in front of the children.) The pastor's whole family just fell apart. A little later, the pastor and his wife got a divorce, and he just disappeared. His wife and the girls stayed in the community. I wonder if that was hard for them. I heard that she eventually remarried. It was my first lesson in the realities that pastors are human, too, and that things are not always as they seem.

The mission church, Prince of Peace, was a wonderful experience. We called an enthusiastic young pastor who came to us with his wife and three little children. He was friendly and energetic. The whole family were such nice, ordinary people that we all loved them. The church grew and grew. When that pastor left some years later, probably to take another call, we got two very poor pastors, one after another, and the church declined very quickly, and it has never recovered. My mother still lives in that community, and we always attend church with her when we go to visit her. There are never more than about twenty-five worshippers. One woman is usually there, a woman I knew well when I attended Prince of Peace. She is just a little older than me, and she is by far the youngest member there. The average age is about that of my mother, in the eighties. The church has no Sunday school or Luther League. Worship is the only activity. I don't know how they support themselves. They do run a day care facility, and perhaps that helps to pay the bills. It is very sad.

Growing up in those two churches was good for me, though. I always had a good feeling about my relationship with the Lord. We memorized a lot of scripture, and I always remember John 3:16. I felt His love. When I was older, I got a better understanding of grace. Basically, I had a happy childhood. I loved going to church. My aunts and uncles and all our friends were there. We always went. It is just what we did, and we were always eager to go. My parents were very involved in the church. My dad was an usher and he served on the church council often, as well as on various church committees. Circle was the center of my mother's life. She was always sewing quilts, both at home and at church, and always doing things for people in need and for various relief projects. Church was a big part of our lives.

Nowadays I think the church is too soft. We don't want to step on anyone's toes, or get tough, or talk about right and wrong. We want to be nice. We don't want to take a stand.

In some ways the church is the same as it was back then. Our worship service has stayed pretty much the same. I like that. I like a traditional service, the reverence and dignity of it. In some ways the church is better. I like that the women usher now and serve on council and committees. But on matters of morality in the church and in the society, I am very disappointed in our church today. These things are very troubling.

HOLY CROSS LUTHERAN CHURCH OXFORD, MICHIGAN

The first church I remember was Holy Cross Lutheran, a Missouri Synod church in Oxford, Michigan, a town of approximately 3,000 population. Oxford is in Oakland County, near Detroit and Flint. Our congregation was about 250 persons, half blue collar factory workers and about half shopkeepers and professionals who serviced the town. I was a member there from 1955-69, confirmed and married there.

My family were faithful attenders. Dad was the church financial secretary for years, and also the janitor—in addition to his job as a tool and dye worker. Mom taught Sunday school and was active in Ladies' Aid. They enjoyed working and serving in the church. I saw that other adults there did, too.

We had two pastors during my childhood. The first was apparently unsatisfactory, because I know that the congregation asked him to leave. The next pastor was wonderful. He was not a particularly great preacher, but he was a warm people person and a good Bible teacher. He taught a Sunday evening Bible class in various homes which my parents attended faithfully and clearly enjoyed.

I was generally bored with the preaching, but I remember a statement from a Christmas sermon which I recall in times of trouble even now. The pastor said that the Bible says of the events around Jesus' birth that the gospel records that they "came to pass; not that they came to stay". I think of that now when I am overwhelmed—this will pass, it isn't here to stay. I understood even as a child that scripture was *true* in a literal sense. I understood very well the way of salvation, but at that time it was head knowledge, not heart knowledge. It was later that I understood salvation and my relationship with Christ in a personal way.

When I was a very young teenager, I was allowed to help with the Easter breakfast at church. It was a revelation. Everybody working together was so friendly, and they accepted me and my help in a way that made me feel very adult. I loved it! I felt like a part of the adult world, and I saw it, even then, as an opportunity for servanthood. That shaped my vocation in the church from that time.

Dad painted the church one year, and I asked him why he was painting the church instead of doing some work somewhere else. I knew we needed the money, but I wondered why he took that job at the church. He told me it was because he loved God and he loved taking care of His church. We did not have family devotions, and though we all were very active in the church, my parents didn't usually talk about their faith with us. That was his way of speaking of his faith to me.

I was married at Holy Cross. During the wedding rehearsal, I approached the altar. I had never been in the chancel, and I guess I was just curious. The pastor talked to my dad about that. Women were not supposed to approach the altar. My father told me about the conversation, but he didn't seem too concerned. I think he didn't think it was as bad as the pastor did. To this day, women are not allowed near the altar in Missouri Synod churches.

The church I attend now is about seven times the size of Holy Cross, so the size difference alone is a great change from the church of my youth. Holy Cross was cozier, more like an extended family. For example, everybody in the church shopped at the Gambles Store because the owner was a member. I find though that with each year at my present church, I feel more at home, so perhaps that family feeling is a product of time as well as size. My ELCA church is much more tolerant than Holy Cross. That's both positive and negative. I'm glad we're more tolerant of individuals, but on subjects like homosexuality, I don't think we should even be talking about it. The scripture is so clear. There's nothing to debate. But we need to be tolerant of the individual homosexual—that is, we need to welcome them. I think the church today is too much like the culture. We in the church do not separate ourselves enough from the culture. And I think the church gives us very little help with dealing with the culture in Christian terms. I think we don't do very much as a church to build faith.

I think the people in the pews today, as in my youth, try to be faithful to God, and to live that.

NATHANIEL LUTHERAN CHURCH
RESERVE, MONTANA

Nathaniel Lutheran is a country church. When I was growing up, in 1946 through the early sixties, the church was often full on a Sunday morning. About two hundred people attended regularly. Today, chiefly because of demographics, about fifty people worship each Sunday. Farms there are bigger than they were fifty years ago, and fewer people live in the area. The members were mostly farmers, and all ethnically Danish. I don't think they'd let anyone in who wasn't Danish. Services were held in Danish until 1956, when it was no longer possible to get a Danish-speaking pastor. When some of the smaller synods merged in 1968, Nathaniel became part of the LCA.

The pastor I remember best was a wonderful man. He was quite blind. I remember how closely he held the Bible when he read from it. Everybody loved the pastor. He knew all of H. C. Andersen's fairy tales by heart, and he used to tell them around the campfire when we had Bible camp.

The liturgy was very much as it is now. We used the old Danish hymnal, and the little black Danish hymnal with just the words, no music, is still in the pews at Nathaniel, still used.

Our whole life centered around the church. The church was the center of social life. In the summer we had midsummer fest, when visiting pastors (they all had to speak Danish) came and held meetings all day Saturday and Sunday. I guess you would call them revival meetings. The Vollmer Church nearby cooperated with us for those meetings. They are still held there.

Our church had its very own Bible camp every summer. Across the road from the church was a parsonage that was no longer occupied. The girls stayed in the parsonage and the boys stayed in tents pitched on the lawn around it. This also was a cooperative effort of the Vollmer Church and Nathaniel Lutheran. We cooked there and had gymnastics, games, crafts and Bible stories. One of our teachers, a lady from the congregation, told stories about missionaries, and we were mesmerized. These Bible camps are still held every summer, and my children went to them when they were younger.

Later, when we were in Luther League, we went to a Bible camp for older children in Denmark, Wisconsin. Luther League was fun at home, too. We played games and had Bible studies and sang a lot.

I thought everybody was Lutheran when I was growing up. Everybody I knew was. So we didn't think too much about how Lutherans were different from other people. We knew we didn't have to eat fish on Friday, and that Catholics did.

We attend the Nathaniel church when we are at the farm today, and otherwise we attend a church near our home in town. Church is different now. We don't have the family sense about it we once had; the camaraderie is gone. People are too busy, I think. The churches in our area of Montana are growing. The population is expanding, and so are the churches. Our particular church is shrinking, and I think it is because the pastor is more or less unavailable. One year, instead of holding confirmation classes weekly for a year or so, he took the kids to Bible camp for a week and called it confirmation class. A lot of people left the church over that. People leave, too, when they don't believe what the pastor believes.

OUR SAVIOR'S LUTHERAN CHURCH
SPRING VALLEY, MINNESOTA

In 1940, when I was born, my folks attended a German Lutheran church in town—Zion Lutheran. There was also a Norwegian Lutheran church, Trinity, in our town. In 1950, those two churches merged and formed Our Savior's Lutheran Church. This merger was worked out a very short time after World War II when there was still a lot of animosity toward Germany. My father was very active in the German church, and also in the negotiations that resulted in the merged church. It was, I think, an unusual merger, and very successful. Most everybody in the two churches went along with the merger. Zion had about 300 members and Trinity had perhaps 150. When I left home in 1958, just eight years after that merger, there were about 550 members at Our Savior's. The church is about 900 members today. In 2001 we celebrated the 100th anniversary of Zion Lutheran, and the 50th anniversary of Our Savior's.

Spring Valley was a town of about 2500 when I was growing up. The church was in town. It served the farming community in the area and the business families who ran the dairy, implement store and other businesses that mostly served the agricultural community. Spring Valley is about 25 miles from Rochester, Minnesota. The growth in Spring Valley today is largely due to an influx of people who work at the Mayo Clinic in Rochester. The clinic runs two buses to Spring Valley each morning and evening to provide transportation for employees to the clinic.

The pastor who confirmed me came to our church in 1950 and stayed ten or twelve years. I was sometimes bored by the sermons, but sometimes the sermons were scholarly and sometimes very inspiring. I think he was a good pastor, particularly for his success in melding the two congregations. Of course there were some people who compared him unfavorably to earlier pastors, but I knew him as a good Christian. He emphasized separation from the Catholics. We were warned that it was a bad idea to date Catholics. He was also against drinking, and he taught us that. Under him, I took confirmation very seriously. We heard a lot of "Thou shalt nots". We also had a lot of memorization. On the two Sundays before our confirmation, the class sat in a row at the front of the church and we were examined in front of the whole congregation. A lot of what I learned at that time comes forth now.

Church was the center of our activities. We had athletic banquets, mother-daughter and father-son banquets, graduation parties—all at the church. My father served on the church council and Mother sang in the choir. Father also taught Sunday School. They supported the church enthusiastically. They gave and participated. There was a family feeling there generally. The kids I was closest to in school were kids I knew at church. When I was growing up the school had release time one morning a week. The kids went to their individual churches for instruction. Those kids who weren't members of a church had study hall, and that was kind of boring, so some of those kids chose a church and went with us.

I also remember a time when we had a revival meeting that lasted every evening from Sunday night through Friday. I particularly remember the pastor, a Pastor Lee who was in a wheelchair. He really got my attention. I was about 14 at the time. It was mostly a revival within our congregation—not so much to bring new people in. There was a parish worker in our church when I was in high school, a young man who had some college training, but no seminary. He called on members, taught Sunday School and helped with the youth. He took an interest in me. It really meant a lot to me. He even took me to Minneapolis to visit the Lutheran Bible Institute in Minneapolis when I was a senior. It overwhelmed me. The idea that I might go to that school overwhelmed me. I visited him later. He eventually went to seminary and became a pastor. He went out of his way for me, and I always remember that, and I am grateful for his concern.

Today it seems to me that the church is more of a social gathering and has a less religious tone. I don't think the Bible and the scriptures are as central to the church as they were in the past. The church seems afraid to speak out about abortion, homosexuality, etc., instead of saying what God's Word says. Music is very important to most Lutheran churches now, and I sometimes think the music program is better supported than our missionaries are. We do less for missions than we used to. In terms of worship and ritual, those are much the same. If my father were living and could worship with us today, I think he would be comfortable.

One thing is better. I remember when my church at home published the amounts each member gave in offerings—names and amounts. That was a bad idea, and of course we don't do that today.

Today I think the Lutheran church is conforming to the world rather than transforming the world. Based on the church's direction and planned direction, the church has been hijacked by ultra-liberals who are more interested in being politically correct than Biblically correct.

Pella Lutheran Church
Omaha, Nebraska

Pella Lutheran in Omaha, United Evangelical Lutheran Church, was always a city church. The congregation worshipped in four different buildings during my childhood. The first was a pretty brick church on 30th and Corby streets. That church was sold to a black Lutheran congregation, and the congregation moved to a white clapboard building on 52nd and Dodge streets. Omaha is very hilly, and the church on 52nd street sat high above the street. As a little girl, I thought there were a hundred steps up to it. We probably rented that facility, for we didn't stay there very long. Next we purchased an unfinished church on 41st and Farnam streets. We didn't move into it right away, for we had a building project. We would put a beautiful church atop the basement already there. Until that was completed, we worshipped and held Sunday School classes in the Admiral theater just a block away. That was very strange, for even on a sunny morning, a theater is a theater, and it was very dark. And then, in less than a year, we moved into the church itself, and it seemed very grand. It still stands there and serves a congregation which is probably seen as an "inner city" church today. That was my home congregation from 1938 until 1959 when I was married there, and moved away the next week.

I don't know how many members we had, but my guess is perhaps two hundred. About half of them were first or second generation immigrants from Denmark. An aunt and uncle and two cousins plus several of my father's cousins and their families as well as many people who had been lifelong friends of my parents were lifelong members.

I don't remember Rev. Kierkegaard who baptized me, and I have only vague memories of Rev. Rasmussen who was our pastor after that. The one vivid memory I have of him is in the foyer of the church on 52nd Street. He had just climbed all those steps on a cold and snowy morning. He stomped his feet to get rid of the snow and took off his fogged-up glasses. Several people were standing around talking and laughing as people do on snowy mornings. Someone asked if it were true that he was going to marry Sophie Jensen, and he smiled and said he was. He was old at the time, I thought, but I was a child, so my perception is questionable. The memory stuck because I had never seen him without his glasses, I had never seen him laughing, and I couldn't imagine anybody that old getting married. After Rev. Rasmussen, Rev. M. G. Christensen came to serve our church. He was the pastor who instructed and confirmed me. Rev. Christensen was a personal gift to me, for he encouraged me to think of college, he honed my intelligence, and he introduced me to great music and literature. Through him I saw possibilities I had never dared to dream of. He was solid on scripture and Lutheran belief, and no one left his confirmation classes without a good understanding of the catechism as well as a good background in scripture. He also drilled it into our heads that it would be a fate worse than death to marry a Catholic. He was the most thoroughly educated person in our church. I wonder sometimes, how he survived there, but he did, for a long time.

When our family visited our Methodist cousins on the farm and went to Sunday School with them, I saw that those children didn't know nearly as much scripture, or even about scripture, as we did. Pella used Concordia Sunday school materials, and I still remember fondly the beautiful full-color Sunday school pamphlets we got every Sunday, with a picture on the front, a paraphrase of a Bible story (for little ones) on the inside, as well as some study questions.

The UELC was a Danish synod, heir to some pietistic notions and to the hymns and some of the philosophy of Grundtvig. I know that now, from my study. At the time, it was just what we were. Until M.G. Christensen's time, our pastors wore no robes, and the abbreviated liturgy was spoken, not sung. We sang a lot of hymns, accompanied by an electronic organ. The organist also played for the hockey games (the Western Hockey League was big in Omaha) and at roller rinks around town. The rumor was that he drank a fair bit between Sundays. When we got choir robes and the choir started processing down the aisle at the beginning of the service, many of the old Danes were disgruntled, including my father, and when the pastor started wearing a stole and surplice, it was taken as an omen that we were on our way back to Rome.

As I grew up, Luther League and Bible camp were highlights of my childhood. Luther League in our church was for all confirmed, unmarried people, and some of the leaguers were in their late twenties. That was wonderful for those of us who were younger. It was our passage into the adult world. It was also handy, because the older fellows could drive us to various activities, and our parents saw them as chaperones, which they were.

The church was the center of our social life. We had smørrebrod suppers (Danish open-faced sandwiches) in the way we have potluck suppers now. I remember an ice cream social and a big Sunday school picnic every summer. I carry a scar inside my lower lip from the time when one of the men rode the teeter-totter with me and lost his balance, dropping to the ground. The force of his fall threw me off the teeter-totter and onto the metal support. He felt terrible, but we all survived just fine.

Wedding receptions at Pella were cake, ice-cream, punch and coffee affairs. And that's how mine was.

The church *is* different today. One difference is the increase in the liturgy. I like the liturgy, but I don't think it should dominate the service. Because of the amount of liturgy and having communion every Sunday, we sing less, now, and the sermons are shorter. There are still some good preachers around. The last two in the parish we belong to have been excellent. But visiting Lutheran churches can be a very disappointing activity. There's a lot of C- preaching out there. I grew up with a congregational style, low-church, Bible-studying bunch of old Lutherans, and in the end I think they had a lot right.

ST. PAUL'S ENGLISH EVANGELICAL LUTHERAN GRAND ISLAND, NEBRASKA

The church of my childhood was St. Paul's English Evangelical Lutheran Church, part of the UELC synod. It was formed for English-speaking people, mostly of German origin, in Central Nebraska. Some years ago, the name was changed to St. Paul's English Lutheran Church. The name does not refer to Englishmen, but to an English-language church at a time when immigrants were beginning to speak the language of the land. The first pastor, who arrived in 1882 on a freight train (so the records say) was called specifically because he was fluent in English. I was a member there from my birth in 1937 until I married in 1959. In the forties it had about 1500 members. In 1982, I know there were 2600. The church became part of the ALC in that merger, and is an ELCA church today. The church was strategically located on Main Street, which is Highway 30 through Nebraska. It was the first brick church in Grand Island. St Paul's when I was growing up was mostly a middle-class church, business and professional people and a few farmers.

The preaching was always very Biblical. We always had all three lessons on Sunday, and the lessons exactly matched the lessons at the Catholic Church in town. I know that because my father was Catholic. Every Sunday he drove Mother and the rest of us to the Lutheran church. Then he went to mass, and picked us up after church. I often asked him what the lessons were, and I was always surprised that they were just the same. I asked him if he understood the lessons. "Weren't they in Latin?" And of course he laughed and said "No, silly, they were in English." The service was liturgical, and I liked it.

St. Paul's was very forward thinking. In about 1957 or 8 it offered a drive-in church service at the local drive-in theater. A lot of people really enjoyed that. There were usually 200-300 cars that came. It was done through the local Council of Churches, but our pastor always had the sermon.

In confirmation class we had to memorize the whole small catechism. There were about twenty in our class. Confirmation classes lasted nine months, every Saturday of the school year, and on Sundays at Sunday School. I had a wonderful Sunday School teacher, a lawyer, who made us memorize Bible verses, and at the end of the year, gave us each a book of one hundred famous poems. I still have it.

My faith was established in those years.

Church today is different. I think it is too liberal. We used to be more structured. Our church had kneeling benches, and I think that created a sense of reverence that I miss now. Confirmation classes are three years now, instead of one. I think that's good. I don't know how it's taught now, because my children are grown. I taught confirmation when our kids were growing up, and I think the other teachers and I did a good job. I like the fact that the church reaches out more than it did in my childhood. I like the emphasis on World Hunger and the Habitat for Humanity project. It seems that extended families don't pitch in to help each other as much as they once did, so they go to agencies for help. I don't think that's good, but I see that the church has to be part of that.

TRINITY LUTHERAN CHURCH
AKRON, IOWA

I'll bet you didn't know there was an Akron in Iowa. When I was growing up the town had about 1300 population and about 200 of them belonged to Trinity Lutheran Church, which was a German congregation. I was a member there from 1924 to 1953, when I got married. Akron was a farming community, and the members of Trinity were farmers and the merchants from the town.

Our pastor preached Hell and brimstone sermons, and we loved it. We listened to him. The preaching was biblical, always biblical. He wasn't paid much. A lot of his income was in barter. He visited the parishioners regularly, and he often went home with eggs or chickens or butter. I think we learned the basics of salvation, though, from our parents. Confirmation classes, including the catechism, were taught by the pastor. I have good memories of that, and the lessons stayed with me. It was instilled into me that Lutherans are different—that they have the purest interpretation of God's will. Luther tried to "clean" the church in his day, and we inherited that.

The church was the center of our social life. Everybody worked in the church, especially the women. They taught Sunday School and worked on projects in Ladies Aid. We had a lot of fun at church. I thought my teachers were so nice; many were my mother's friends. They told us Bible stories and we had to remember them. When we were in confirmation class, the whole class had to sit in one or two pews right in front, right under the pastor's nose. If you dozed off, he would wake you up, right during the sermon, and none of the parents complained either. The pastor was a stern fellow. All of the services were in German for many years. I was the youngest of six children, and the first child in our family who was confirmed in English. I always sort of regretted that. Our parents talked to us in German, but all of our education was in English.

The church is very lax now, especially in recent years. The Bible is interpreted to fit society rather than otherwise. I've even heard bishops say that the Bible needs to be reinterpreted according to our lifestyles today. Isn't that stupid? However, I think that the pure teaching is still there. There are still good preachers who teach the Word purely. But mostly in sermons the everlasting life is overshadoweed by the secular life.

Regardless of the humps and bumps in the church these days, I still choose to be a Lutheran, although I know that being a Lutheran is not the most important thing. Traditionalism doesn't save you.

Trinity Lutheran Church
Greencastle, Pennsylvania

Our little church had about one hundred members. It had split off from the big Lutheran church in town before I was born. Mom went to church more than Dad. He usually had to work. But none of us went all that much. I do remember Luther League, and I was confirmed in that church. I remember one pastor particularly because I cleaned his house once. I can't think why I did that, but there were eleven of us kids, and we all worked whenever we could, so that might explain it. It might have been when he was moving. He and his wife were wonderful people. Everybody liked them, and I have good memories of him.

The church was mostly older people. I wonder how they managed to support themselves.

The Bible study I remember was in a lady's house near us. I'm not even sure she was a member of our church. We had to memorize the books of the Bible in order, and we were given a verse to memorize each week. At the end of that class we were each given a white zippered Bible. I'll never forget that. I went to Sunday school more after I was about ten years old.

I learned in my childhood that God created the heavens and the earth. Somehow we learned that we'd grow up and get married and have children and be faithful to our husbands and wives. We knew that was important.

When I was out of high school, I married and we didn't go to church very often. My husband just was not a church person. That marriage ended. When I married again, it was in the church I belong to now. I loved the pastor who married us. I joined the church right away. My husband and I took the Bethel Bible Series class a few years ago. I thought it was wonderful. "We are blessed to be a blessing." That stays with me. We also went to the Holy Land with our pastor awhile ago. We learned so much and it made the Bible so real. I'd like to do that again, but it seems too dangerous just now.

My church today is much better than the one I grew up in. It means a lot to me. I think that's because I am more involved in it. I've been very happy with it. I'm worried now, though, about the problems with the ELCA. I don't know what's going to happen to us with the business of ordaining homosexuals and so on.

Zion Lutheran Church
LaVerne, Minnesota

Zion Lutheran was a Lutheran Free Church of 150-175 members during the years 1928-1955. There were four Lutheran churches in LaVerne, and they were all filled with immigrants every Sunday. My parents, too, were immigrants from Norway who had not been too happy with the state church. That is why they belonged to the Free Church, which was less formal. We didn't have choir robes or special clothes for the pastor, and our services were mostly the reading of scripture, the sermon and singing. I also think that the folks were more comfortable among the simpler folk of the Free Church. Our church members were farmers and the business people of the town. There were no professional people in the congregation. There came a time when the national church wanted to eliminate the smaller churches and the Norwegian speaking churches; they wanted them to join together in larger congregations. My folks really fought that.

When I was growing up we had good pastors, and the church was full. Later I went away to teach, and when I returned to get married there were very few people in church. It was embarrassing. After that pastor resigned the pastor who came really helped the church grow. He was very human, biblically oriented, very well educated and cultured, and very warm. He gave wonderful sermons. By that time the church had changed to English. They dropped the Norwegian in 1944. But the point is that the pastor makes a big difference.

By and large, the congregation was quite unified. My mother was a healer. I can remember her speaking in a very kind way that helped people get over difficulties. It was a great gift. But the church was mostly unified.

One thing I remember very fondly. I had learned to play the piano by ear, and the church recognized the need for music, so they came to me and offered to pay me to play for services. I was very surprised. I wouldn't let them. I wanted to play as a service. And so that was how it was.

The Christmas festivals at church were grand Norwegian affairs, with hymns around the Christmas tree. I was lucky that my Norwegian heritage as well as my faith were part of my childhood in that church. That has stayed with me.

How is the church different today? We attended a church for twenty-five years where we live now, and the pastor never once spoke of sin. It was, love covers everything. People need leadership. Later we saw our church split over the charismatic movement. That was a terrible time. Again, the pastor was a nice man, but the sermons were pale, and the pentecostal element tore the church apart. With the right pastor, though, the Lutheran church is still biblical. The music has changed and some of that is all right. You have to appeal to the young people. But it has to remain Lutheran. I don't like the new hymns coming out that sing of our mother God, and I don't like changing the wording to get rid of the *he*.

A good thing, though, is that now people dare to speak up and peacefully disagree in the church. We used to respect the pastors and missionaries so much that we didn't dare to criticize. So many of them were unapproachable. That is a change for the better.

NOTES

1. Strommen, Merton P., "The Church and Homosexuality: Searching for a Middle Ground," 2nd Edition, Revised, Kirk House Publishers, Minneapolis, Minnesota, 2001, p. 96.
2. Dallas, Joe, *Update Magazine,* August 1996.
3. Strommen, p. 28
4. Nestingen, James A., *Is There a Law? The Lutheran Reformation and Homosexual Practice,* "Christian Sexuality: Normative and Pastoral Principles," edited by Russell E. Saltzman, Kirk House Publishers, Minneapolis, Minnesota, 2003, p. 32.
5. Strommen, p. 27
6. Neuhaus, Richard John, "The Public Square, Sexual and Related Disorders," *First Things,* March 2003, p. 68-69
7. Strommen, p. 27
8. Eberstadt, Mary, "The Family: Discovering the Obvious," *First Things,* February 2004, p. 10-12.
9. Gagnon, Robert J., *Does the Bible Regard Same-Sex Intercourse as Intrinsically Sinful?,* "Christian Sexuality:Normative and Pastoral Principles, p. 113.
10. Nestingen, James A., *Is There a Law? The Lutheran Reformation and Homosexual Practice,* Christian Sexuality: Normative and Pastoral Principles," p. 37.
11. Neuhaus, Richard John, "The Public Square, While We're At It," *First Things,* October 2004, p.88.
12. Mills, David, "Deadly Bureaus," *Touchstone: A Journal of Mere Christianity,* September 2004, p. 39.
13. Grindal, Gracia, "WordAlone Members Working on a New Hymnal," *WordAlone Network News,* September-October, Vol. 5, No. 5, p. 9.
14. Forde, Gerhard O., "Where God Meets Man: Luther's Down-to-Earth Approach to the Gospel, Augsburg Publishing House, Minneapolis, Minnesota, l972, p. 72.
15. Forde, Gerhard O., p. 94.

Printed in the United States
24322LVS00004B/148-171